HISTORIC AMERICA

The Northwest

HISTORIC AMERICA

The Northwest

Jim Kaplan

THUNDER BAY
P·R·E·S·S
SAN DIEGO, CALIFORNIA

Above: *An agile worker tops a spar tree for Clear Lake Lumber Co., Washington (1919).*

Page 1*: Punchbowl Falls on Eagle Creek, in the Columbia River Gorge, Oregon.*

Page 2*: Seattle's distinctive skyline, seen at dusk from Queen Anne Hill.*

Page 6*: Crystal Crag reflected in Lake George, in California's Sierra Nevada.*

SERIES EDITOR: John S. Bowman
EDITOR: Sara Hunt
ASSOCIATE EDITOR: Robin Langley Sommer
PHOTOGRAPHY: Ed Cooper
ART DIRECTOR: Nikki L. Fesak
EDITORIAL ASSISTANT: Deborah Hayes

Thunder Bay Press
An imprint of the
Advantage Publishers Group
5880 Oberlin Drive
San Diego, CA 92121-4794
www.advantagebooksonline.com

Copyright © 2002 Saraband (Scotland) Ltd.

All notations of errors or omissions should be addressed to Thunder Bay Press, editorial department, at the above address. All other correspondence (author inquiries, permissions) concerning the content of this book should be addressed to Saraband, The Arthouse, 752–756 Argyle Street, Glasgow G3 8UJ, Scotland, hermes@saraband.net.

ISBN 1-57145-713-5

Library of Congress Cataloging-in-Publication Data available upon request.

Printed in China
1 2 3 4 5 06 05 04 03 02

Acknowledgments and Photo Credits
The publisher would like to thank all who assisted in the production of this book, including those listed at left, and: Erin Pikor, for the original jacket design; Deborah Hayes, for compiling the gazetteer and index; Debby Cooper; Simon Saunders. All color photographs in this volume are the copyright of Ed Cooper, unless otherwise noted by page number in the list below. Grateful acknowledgment is also made to the following individuals and institutions for permission to reproduce illustrations and photographs: © **Ed Cooper**: b/w photographs on pages 35, 102, 106; © **Terry Donnelly**: 2, 10–11, 12–13, 18–19; **The National Archives**: 38, 40, 43r, 46–47, 66, 83t, 86, 90, 91, 95, 119; **Prints and Photographs Division, Library of Congress**: 4, 34, 42–43, 44, 50, 51, 54, 82 (both), 83b, 87, 94 (both), 98, 99, 107b, 111, 114, 115, 122; **Lane County Historical Museum**: 74, 103; **Collection of Glenn O. Myers**: 48; **Collection of Frank Oppel**: 58; **Collection of Peter Palmquist**: 110; **Planet Art**: 62; **Yale University Map Collection, photograph © Joseph Szaszfai**: 55, 63, 85.

TABLE OF CONTENTS

INTRODUCTION

This is a book about the Northwest, which we define here as comprising Washington, Oregon, and northern California. "The Northwest" is often regarded as including Idaho, even Montana, but the editors of the *Historic America* series have assigned these states to another volume, "The Mountain States," because of several natural and historical features. As for including northern California—well, anyone in the state will tell you that northern and southern California belong in different regions, if not different worlds altogether! We intend to demonstrate why California, from Monterey north to the Oregon border, belongs properly to the Northwest.

Because of its remoteness from the major population centers in the East, the Northwest was long the least explored area of the country. Even today, "Northwest" inspires precious few word associations for people who haven't been there: Seattle—rain, high tech, latté; San Francisco—rain, hippies, latté; Portland—rain, bookstores, latté. Yet the region actually holds great diversity and positively teems with extraordinary beauty, bountiful natural resources, and fascinating history. Newcomers are often struck dumb by what they see. Students are invariably intrigued by what they read.

Washington, Oregon, and northern California have much in common. For one thing, they're new, geologically speaking, and have been—in fact still are!—subject to sudden violent change. Evidence of geological instability is everywhere, from the San Francisco earthquake of 1906 (and other, less serious earthquake activity since) to Oregon's Crater Lake, almost 2,000 feet deep; and from California's Lava Beds

National Monument to dramatic Mount St. Helens, whose eruption in 1980 spewed volcanic dust all over eastern Washington and northern Idaho. The Cascade Range extends down the entire region from north to south. Strange, wonderful rivers run through the whole area as well. In northern California, these spread out like the fingers of a hand, while Washington and Oregon are separated by the majestic Columbia River. Second only to the Mississippi-Missouri river system in size, the 1,210-mile Columbia has a drainage area of 259,000 square miles. It rises in Canada and descends into Washington, then, fed by tributaries

Page 7: North Head Light (1898), which guards the entrance to the Columbia River, near Long Beach, Washington.

Opposite: A tranquil view of Mount St. Helens, Washington, before its devastating 1980 eruption.

Below: Tufa towers— formed of mineral deposits—at California's Mono Lake.

from as far away as Montana and Idaho, it flows westward to the sea. All along its course are cliffs, falls, canyons, and lakes. While temperatures in northern California can soar in the summer and plummet in winter, Washington and Oregon are more temperate regions, with snow largely restricted to the mountaintops. And yes, much of the region does indeed experience the volume of rainfall so often associated with it, because of the mountain ranges close to the Pacific Coast, which block moisture from the eastern part of the area.

A second similarity shared by northern California, Oregon, and Washington is cultural. It probably can be traced back to the frontier mentality of escape from Eastern pretensions. Whenever or however it began, the counter-cultural movement that emerged in San Fran- cisco (never call it "Frisco" unless you want to be marked out as a rank tourist!) of the 1960s migrated up to Eugene, Oregon, and then on to other parts of the Northwest, where grandma dresses, pony tails, and '73 Volkswagons found new life. In fact, northern California is so "laid back" that when a visiting Eastern lawyer asked a San Francisco secretary to work late, she replied, "It's not my style." Nor are Oregonians or Washingtonians obsessed with ten-to twelve-hour workdays— except, perhaps, for those working in a relatively few high-pressure jobs. Indeed, at this writing, many transplanted Easterners, among others, regard the Northwest as a vacationland as much as a job fair.

Certainly the region is among the country's most beautiful. In Oregon, mountains slope down to the 296-mile craggy coastline, all of which is open to the public. The combination of dunes and seacaves is probably unparalleled in all North America. In central Oregon, around the mountains known as The Three Sisters, are seventeen glaciers— an extraordinary field so far south of the polar ice cap. Indeed, Oregon's interior is home to endless subtle attractions, as befits a region in which camels once roamed. "No region on earth shows more abundant marine fossils than the Willamette Valley, which was ideally arranged to become a great aquarium," George W. Fuller wrote in *A History of the Pacific Northwest*.

At the climax of the last Ice Age, some 20,000 years ago, the ice cap reached down as far as uppermost northern Washington. As it receded, flowing water left behind 675 glaciers—fully two-thirds of the total in the forty-eight contigu-

Pages 10–11: Grasslands and sage under the dramatic basalt cliffs at Drumheller Channels Natural Landmark, in the Columbia National Wildlife Refuge, Washington. As the last Ice Age came to an end, the tremendous force of the floodwaters eroded the volcanic basalt in this region, creating remarkable formations in the landscape.

Pages 12–13: Morning light over Eagle Cap Peak and Sunshine Lake, in the Wallowa-Whitman National Forest in northeastern Oregon, part of the canyon country carved by the Snake River.

Left: Mount St. Helens, still smoking after the May 18, 1980, eruption that blew 1,314 feet from the top of the mountain, which now stands at 8,363 feet high. The blast left a 2,000-foot-deep crater, and its violent emission of boiling lava caused 57 human deaths and killed an estimated 7,000 big game animals, while thrusting into the atmosphere sufficient smoke to encircle the globe within fifteen hours.

ous states—in what is now the state of Washington. The combination of glacial-fed lakes and rivers and the mountains can mesmerize a newcomer. "When the sun shone and the clouds broke during early fall, there were spectacular views," says Andrea Bierstein, a lawyer who has spent two years in Seattle. "Twenty years later, I can still remember driving north over a bridge near Lake Union, and it seemed there were water and mountains everywhere, Elliott Bay and the Olympic Mountains to my left and the Cascades to my right. I had to catch my breath and keep my eye on the road." Other views could be every bit as entrancing as this: "Camping in the rain forest on the Olympic Peninsula, I saw a huge herd of elk emerge from the fog at 5:00 AM," says Bierstein.

Northwesterners have not simply enjoyed their natural beauty, they've also fought to protect it. The more the Northwest developed, the more it conserved. This was possible in part because the region didn't fill up quickly. East of the Cascade Range—which is to say, in most of Washington and Oregon—are plains that support only a few substantial cities like Spokane, Washington. Travelers who drive the 250 miles north between Sacramento, California, and the Oregon border still find only one city, Redding, with more than 50,000 residents. Following the lead of California's Yosemite National Park, which in 1864 became the first site to receive a federal grant of conservation for public use, northern California, Oregon, and Washington added dozens of other protected spaces during the twentieth century. You can take your pick: Redwood National Park along northern California's seacoast; the

1.1-million-acre Mount Hood National Forest in northern Oregon, with its hot springs, waterfalls, meadows, and lakes; or snow-capped Olympic National Park in Washington, to name only a few.

Northwestern nature includes some animal wonders, as well. Any discussion of wildlife must begin with the beaver, the original attraction to the region for most non-natives. When its pelts became fashionable in both eastern America and western Europe for hats, coats, cuffs, collars, and linings, trappers flooded in to exploit the area, and the

Opposite: The majestic Pacific Coast and volcanic basalt cliffs above the beach at Ecola State Park, Oregon.

Below: Crater Lake, Oregon, with red volcanic rock in the foreground.

Right: Moss creeps over these fallen alders on the near-silent floor of Quinault Rainforest, Olympic National Park, Washington. This part of the Pacific Northwest contains two-thirds of the world's ancient and very rare temperate rainforests.

Hudson's Bay Company virtually ruled it. As a result of competition primarily between British and American trappers, the beaver was nearly exterminated, along with mink, river otter, wolverine, American bobcat, marten, fisher, and lynx. Fortunately, beaver fur eventually went out of fashion midway through the nineteenth century, and the industrious little creatures survived after all.

The introduction of the horse and the development of firearms allowed hunters to decimate the bison population. Unrestricted hunting also depleted the trumpeter swan, whose feathered skin was treasured along with its meat. And agriculture was a two-pronged threat. On the one hand, it depleted habitat for elk and other animals. On the other, it set livestock and predators at odds. The result was what may be understated as an adversarial attitude toward predators, as expressed by one so-called conservationist, William Hornaday: "At the head of the list of evil-doers stands the Gray Wolf…strong of limb and jaw, a master of cunning and the acme of cruelty…The proper course for a wild gray wolf is to kill it as quickly as possible."

Damming for irrigation and electricity reduced the runs of salmon and steelhead trout swimming upstream to spawn. People were kinder to other species, if often unintentionally. The black-tail deer, for example, actually thrived as a result of forest fires bred by lumbering, because of the shrubby vegetation that spread in their wake. Agriculture gave as well as taking away. The fields of grain fed prairie chicken and grouse, while grazing tended to replace grass with seed fit for quail and doves. By the late nineteenth century, humans were working deliberately to protect species by opening sanctuaries in national parks, charging licensing fees for fishing and hunting, and regulating their kills. But from the beginning, there has been competition between the newly arrived Easterners who wanted to save the wilderness and settled Westerners who wanted to tame it.

The history that unfolds within these pages contains roughly equal parts of neglect, good fortune, epic heroism, and exploitation. Between the time Europeans first sighted the Northwest and the time they settled in, nearly three centuries had elapsed. This neglect stemmed in part from sheer distance. The first Europeans in North America

settled the nearer East Coast, and for good reasons. The trip around South America by sea was costly, time-consuming, and dangerous, while trekking across the continent was quite unimaginable before the Lewis and Clark Expedition of 1804–6. Early explorers who did sail up and down the West Coast were unnerved by its craggy coastline with both shoals and breakers that spelled "graveyard" for so many vessels. The natives were not always welcoming—especially when the Europeans opened fire on them with strange and lethal weapons. Finally, the earliest Europeans weren't interested in the Northwest for settlement purposes:

to them, the attraction was simply the potential last stage of the fabled Northwest Passage that they never found.

Even when the region attracted trappers and traders, only a small miracle could have made much of it appealing to settlers. American history abounds in good fortune, if not pure luck—those outcomes that surpassed all expectations. This was the case with the great expedition led by Meriwether Lewis and William Clark, which opened up the Northwest for large-scale settlement. Who on earth could have expected them to succeed? The band of some forty-five men who set out from St. Louis was vulnerable to the elements, sickness,

Above: Spawning salmon in crystal-clear waters near Juneau, Alaska. Salmon has provided a staple of Northwestern diets from early Native American times onward.

Opposite: Ruby Beach on the Olympic Peninsula, Washington, where weathered lumber is frequently seen washed up on the rugged shores.

find reconsiles all the Indians, as to our friendly intentions—a woman with a party of men is our token of peace."

The expedition had been sent out by President Thomas Jefferson to advance fur trading and geographical knowledge. Thanks in part to contributions from the Charbonneaus and many Native Americans, the party returned with a single loss of life (probably due to a ruptured appendix). Two natives also died in the attempt. But the expedition produced so much interesting data that settlement of the trans-Mississippi West became inevitable. "Their achievement has been called the most perfect of its kind in the history of the world," was the conclusion drawn in *The New Encyclopedia of the American West.*

After this epic adventure, the upper Northwest began filling up with missionaries, and later, with settlers. Good fortune—or perhaps happenstance— also figured in the political history of the region. By all odds, Oregon and Washington should have flown the Union Jack flag, not the Stars and Stripes. They were much closer to British-ruled Canada than to any other settled part of the United States. Though jointly governed by Americans and British in the early days of the Northwest Territory, Oregon and Washington were effectively governed by the Hudson's Bay Company, the powerful British trading and trapping firm. Moreover, partly for compassionate reasons, partly to extend its dominion, the company had helped Americans to settle Oregon's fertile Willamette Valley. Nonetheless, the British firm outraged settlers by besting them in business, securing the loyalty of local Native Americans, and claiming land coveted by American Methodists.

accidents, and enemies. Surely some of them would die of diseases. Surely others would die in the rivers and mountains, or be picked off by unknown tribes. The travelers might well become hopelessly lost, their records and members scattered. Instead, the expedition discovered one of the most celebrated Native Americans in our history: the guide and interpreter Sacagawea. A Lemhi Shoshone who was married to the French-Canadian fur trader Toussaint Charbonneau, she gave the party priceless information on topography and helped Lewis and Clark trade for the horses they needed desperately to cross the great Divide. And that was not all. Wrote Clark: "The wife of Shabono [Charbonneau] our interpetr we

Previous pages:
A farmstead in the
fertile Klickitat Valley,
Washington, with Mt.
Adams rising in the
background.

On May 2, 1843, an open-air meeting in Champoeg, Oregon, that was ostensibly called to discuss the hazards of bears, mountain lions, and wolves, opted instead to pass an American proposal organizing the Pacific Coast's first ever provisional government. Its constitutional rights included freedom of religion, jury trial, a ban on slavery and taxes, and 640 acres for anyone who filed a claim and built a cabin. The momentous action was decided by two votes. One of them came from a French-Canadian who originally feared his cabin's window glass would be taxed by the American government; another French-Canadian eased his concerns. That was it: two French-Canadians won the day on behalf of English-speaking Americans. The Champoeg vote contributed to the establishment of the Oregon Territory in 1848 and to Oregon statehood in 1859. Subsequently, London lost all interest in land south of the 49th parallel. In the words of historian Richard White: "The area north of the Columbia, which Americans had neither first explored nor settled nor conquered, became part of the American West."

But it would be wrong to overstate the importance of luck. Heroism figured every bit as prominently. It was heroic for the Lewis and Clark party to set forth, survive an almost killing winter, and persist in the face of many obstacles. It was heroic for settlers to endure the myriad hazards of the Oregon Trail in their Conestoga wagons. And it was especially heroic for the driven railroad workers heading eastward (from Sacramento, California) and west (from the 100th meridian in Missouri) to connect up their lines at Promontory Point, in Utah, on that memorable May day in 1869. For once, Americans of different ethnic groups worked together effectively. Working their way from the West were 11,000 Chinese immigrants, who labored more efficiently than others, because they arrived in close-knit units all speaking the same dialect, bathed every evening, ate varied diets, and drank only tea made from boiled water. From the East came crews dominated by Irish workers, many of whom had served the Union during the Civil War and were looking for another chance to overcome the prevailing prejudices against them. Among the other groups employed were Mexicans, Germans, Englishmen, ex-Confederate soldiers, and many former slaves. And somehow, enduring brutal working conditions and unimaginable winters, they coexisted for four years to build a lasting monument.

This was the one event that really opened the West. Notwithstanding the movement to Oregon and Washington from the 1830s through to the 1850s, most Americans saw the West Coast as a foreign country, far less accessible than Europe. North and South had become united—at least, officially—after the Civil War. Now East had met West, and the United States effectively became a continent rather than a region. In the words inscribed on a ceremonial spike: "May God continue the unity of our country as this railroad unites the two great oceans of the world." The railroads quickly became fashionable as well as useful. In 1877 the Transcontinental Express carried passengers all the way from New York to San Francisco.

However, it would be misleading to imply that the Northwest was a vast wilderness to be attained only by super-

Left: A barge slides under the bridge that spans the Columbia River at Astoria, Oregon. Originally a fort founded by John J. Astor's Pacific Fur Company, Astoria was the first permanent settlement founded by Americans along the Pacific Coast.

25

Opposite: This historic round barn is a landmark in Santa Rosa, in California's Sonoma County, a region now world-famous for its wines.

Below: The Mariposa County Courthouse (1854) is the oldest still in use in California.

human effort. It had originally been settled by simple, hard-working men (the women did not arrive until later) struggling for riches and survival, but all work and no play would have made them all dull boys indeed. Sports and other pastimes gave them relief from endless toil and the harsh realities of their daily lives. Before succumbing to the obsession with organized sport that would soon grip the entire nation, Northwesterners created their own ingenious new diversions. In logging camps, two men engaged in "birling" contests in which they stood at either end of a waterborne log and spun it until one opponent took an unwelcome bath. Telling "tall tales" involved spinning creative stories, with the man telling the biggest "windy" applauded and the fellow with the biggest repertoire sure to "sing down" his opponents. (It is no coincidence that one of our folklore's best-known "superheroes"— our Paul Bunyan—emerged from the logging camps of the Northwest, while one of our favorite short stories was inspired by Mark Twain's days in northern California, which resulted in "The Celebrated Jumping Frog of Calaveras County.") California skiing dates back to the need for winter transportation to the old mining camps. "Snow skates" running to 10 feet long or more came equipped with toe bindings and a balance pole that could be straddled for braking. Skaters might exceed 60 miles per hour in competition.

Things were not so carefree, however, if you happened to be an "other," whether a Native American, a Mexican, an African American, an Asian, or anyone else who differed from the light-skinned, Protestant majority who considered it their "manifest destiny" to conquer the continent. It didn't have to be that way, and in the beginning it was not. In 1579 Sir Francis Drake anchored off northern California and proclaimed that the natives he met were the princes of the world. He treated them like royalty, too. Drake's instinct was sound. The Northwestern Indians were among the earliest of North Americans to evolve a highly developed social order; and their excellent craftsmanship resulted in elaborate plank houses, twined baskets, cedar canoes, totem poles, woven blankets, and many other artifacts.

Right: The spillways open at the 312-foot-deep concrete-arch O'Shaughnessy Dam across the Tuolumne River in Hetch Hetchy Valley, Yosemite National Park, California. Controversial from the outset, plans for the project prompted naturalist John Muir to exclaim: "Dam Hetch Hetchy? As well dam for water-tanks the people's cathedrals and churches, for no holier temple has ever been consecrated by the heart of man." Muir's writings, together with the sublime photography of Ansel Adams, helped make this valley one of the world's best-known areas of outstanding natural beauty.

Unfortunately Drake was an exception. Other Europeans decimated the Native American population, whether accidentally, through disease, or by deliberate massacre. Historians have searched high and low for balance in the struggle between newcomers and natives, and early chroniclers justified themselves by calling the latter "savages." In the last analysis, the facts show little balance. Despite occasional unwarranted violence, most Indian attacks were reactive rather than provocative. And despite some celebrated massacres that the newcomers sought to avenge, most internecine violence was generated less by fear than by racism and hunger for land and wealth. Perhaps the saddest case described herein is the tragic fate of the Nez Percé, the friendly people who willingly helped settlers and American armies only to be driven 1,500 miles from their homeland.

If the residents of both Oregon and Washington herded Native Americans onto reservations, Californians simply killed them. In a frontier ethic driven by the thirst for mineral wealth and a demand for instant statehood, Indians were just seen as impediments. Miners destroyed the game and fish they had relied upon, effectively starving many to death. Others were killed by disease and forced labor. Hunting parties were sent out, much as the early settlers of Australia pursued the land's aborigines. There were some 150,000 Indians in California before the Gold Rush of 1848–9. By 1870 their numbers had been reduced to 30,000—"the worst slaughter of Indian people in United States history," according to *The West: An Illustrated History*.

Mexicans in California, meanwhile, lost their claims to land, and other groups were segregated and subject to

Opposite: Downtown San Francisco seen from Alamo Square, with the historic "painted ladies" in the foreground.

discriminatory laws. For their part, Oregonians didn't legalize the African-American vote until 1959, and at one point Washingtonians forced their Chinese population out of the state. At last, however, during the second half of the twentieth century, the Northwest became synonymous with genuine progressivism. Portland, Oregon, has led the way in combating urban sprawl. San Francisco has welcomed a large gay community. Washington has elected an Asian-American governor. Today, the region's problems are less those of venal forces preying upon the disempowered than of legitimate concerns clashing with each other. One example is the spotted owl/lumber controversy. One

side argues for the endangered species, the other for a respected profession. On another front, the high-tech movement in northern California changed communications forever, only to decline when overdevelopment—call it too much of a good thing—caused businesses to fail. And in the greatest of ironies, the Northwest's bounty—its mild climate, extraordinary natural wonders, recreational opportunities, fair-play attitudes—has attracted so many immigrants as to risk overpopulation. But as the following pages show, whether you live in it, visit it, or simply want to learn more about it, the Northwest is an exciting and rewarding region with myriad facets all its own.

Right: California's state capitol in Sacramento, built between 1860–74.

Overleaf: A serene moonlit view of Orcas Island rising behind a gillnetter fishing boat in Puget Sound, Washington. Gillnets hang vertically in the water and catch fish in their mesh.

THE
FIRST
INHABITANTS

Previous page: This carving is a detail of a totem pole, typical of several Northwestern tribes. Such figures represent animals or mythological beings with which clans and individuals are often identified.

Below: These Miwok Indians are pictured hunting near the site of the future Spanish mission and city of San Francisco.

The story of the ancestors of the Native Americans who have long inhabited the Northwest belongs to the greater story of the peopling of North America. Its basic outline has long been generally agreed upon: during a period of the last Ice Age—roughly 23,000–13,000 BC—when large quantities of the world's waters were locked up in great ice caps and glaciers, people from Asia made their way across the exposed land bridge known as Beringia (so named because it was really the bed of the Bering Sea) and—by at least 12,000 BC—were beginning to move down through corridors in Alaska and Canada. Almost certainly they were relatives of the various peoples living in northeastern Asia, and they were probably motivated primarily by the search for ready supplies of food. Initially they found this in the great herds and colonies of grazing mammals (including mammoths and giant bison, bears, and beaver) that they pursued deeper and deeper into North America. The search for alternative food sources and more hospitable environments presumably led them still farther south across Middle America and into South America.

Although this has long been the most widely accepted view, respected authorities have recently advanced increasing objections to and variations on this simple version. Certain experts, for instance, believe that—at least complementing the overland migrants—some people set off from the Asian mainland in small boats and made their way along the southern coast of the islands and mainland of Alaska, then down the western coast of Alaska and Columbia, to the shores of present-day Washington and Oregon, if not farther. These people would probably have been attracted by the fish and other abundant sea life along the coasts rather than the land mammals, and from the beginning their mode of life would have differed significantly from that of the inland dwellers. Remains of a man found on Prince of Wales Island off the southern coast of Alaska, for instance, are dated to 9,200 BC and indicate that he lived on seafood.

Perhaps the greatest controversies swirl around the time-frame in which these first inhabitants arrived in the Western hemisphere. (This should not be confused with the arrival of the ancestors of the Aleut and Inuit peoples who today inhabit the arctic and subarctic regions: there is little serious dispute that they came from Siberia and moved across North America in two major waves—the first about 4000 years BC, the second, only about AD 500.) Most of the claims for really ancient sites—some alleged to establish human presence as long ago as 200,000 BC—are in regions well south of the Northwest, although stone tools found in the Old Crow region of the Yukon, close to the border of south-western Alaska, have been claimed as dating to 30,000-25,000 BC. However, most scholars question these claims and would date the oldest remains of the Northwest to much later. They accept as among the earliest evidence of human habitation in this region remains found at Paulina Lake in central Oregon and at the Marmes rock shelter on the Snake River in southeastern Washington, both dated to about 8000 BC.

There is also disagreement over the racial or ethnic makeup of the first individuals to make their way into North America. For many years it was affirmed that they were a relatively small band, all of mongoloid stock—not referring to any fundamental species differences, but to several secondary biological and physical characteristics. Now some authorities believe that whether the first Americans came in one wave or several, they were not exactly like any of the major racial groupings of the modern world.

All such details and debates aside, there is now general agreement that whatever the exact period in which these so-called Paleo-Indians began to settle in the Northwest, they would have faced an environment that was quite different from that known by later Native Americans. The great ice caps and glaciers were only beginning to retreat, and the region would have been considerably colder and wetter. The inland dwellers would have found some rivers that followed different courses in later millennia, and many existing lakes and other bodies of water would eventually dry up. The animal population would have been changing: large mammals like the mammoth would have

been retreating, eventually to die out (whether from overhunting, climate change, or disease), and vegetation was also in transition. It is generally agreed, too, that as the ice caps and glaciers melted and released vast quantities of water back into the ocean, sea levels rose and slowly pushed people farther inland while erasing all traces of earlier human presence along the coasts.

The consensus is that the first inhabitants of the Northwest spent several thousand years engaged in little more than hunting and gathering food. It is now recognized, however, that their diet was quite varied—bison, elk, deer, pronghorn, rabbits, birds, salmon and other fish, berries, nuts (including acorns), and such roots as camas. Along the coast, the inhabitants certainly depended more heavily on seafood—many species of fish, shellfish, whale, and seal. During these first millennia, there was little to distinguish these people from the peoples living across much of North America. Indeed, all these early North American cultures are characterized mainly by the stone projectile points they used for hunting, named, in turn, by the sites in

Above: *This sculpture by Doug van Howd is a life-size (12-foot) mammoth of the type hunted down by the first inhabitants of North America. The statue stands in Mammoth Lakes, California.*

Overleaf: *Mt. Rainier, in Washington. From at least 5000 BC peoples living in its foothills have regarded the summit as sacred. A dormant volcano, its last major eruption was about 500 BC.*

Below: *This Wishram woman is fashioning a basket. Although they lived inland in Washington, the Wishram (or Wishham) shared much of the culture of the Northwest Coast peoples.*

New Mexico where the first types were found: the Clovis culture phase (from about 12,000 BC) followed by the Folsom culture phase (starting about 9500 BC). In parts of the Northwest, local variations of the Folsom stone points are known as Cascade points.

By about 4000 BC, some changes were emerging in the culture of these inhab-

itants of the Northwest. Diet was clearly becoming more varied, as grinding stones and mortars and pestles indicate that at least some people were preparing plant foods. Remains of pit houses indicate that people were settling down, becoming less nomadic. Although there is evidence that inhabitants of the Northwest had been showing reverence

for their dead since at least 8500 BC—burying them with tools, bone ornaments, shells, and other artifacts—now there are signs of cemeteries that indicate villages. Still, it is believed that most people of this period were relatively mobile, moving in small bands from place to place in search of food, or stone for their weapons and tools.

Not until about 1000 BC do we see the first emergence of patterns of human culture anticipating those that would eventually become associated with the Northwest Indian peoples encountered by the first Europeans in this region. Languages were evolving, material cultures were developing, societal arrangements were taking shape. Even so, we must go slowly in speaking of the different tribes or nations that eventually became known to Europeans. There were constant movements, regroupings, migrations, displacements, even extinctions. Some of the tribes known to Europeans in historic times, in fact, appear to have moved up into the Northwest from the south. These people moved here and there for all kinds of reasons, but there is no denying that some tribes were more aggressive than others and pushed intruders out of their territories. At the very least, we can say that these early Native Americans did not observe the national, state, or even natural boundaries we now impose. Above all, the names of the many so-called nations, tribes, and other groups have changed greatly over the centuries: the historic and modern names often tell us nothing about who these people were thousands of years ago. But by 1000 BC, we can at least claim that the inhabitants of the Northwest could be classified into two basic cultures—coastal and inland.

COASTAL PEOPLES

The Native Americans who lived along the coast would develop a highly distinctive culture based on the specific environment that prevailed from the northwestern coast of Alaska all the way down to northern California, a distance of well over 2,000 miles. The terrain is dominated by a mountainous spine, with slopes that often drop sharply down to the sea and elsewhere allow for a narrow strip of coastal land that never becomes much wider than 150 miles. The coastline is marked by numerous inlets, offshore islands, and countless rivers and streams. Thus from the beginning, the inhabitants of this coast depended heavily on seafood, especially salmon, but also many other fish, shellfish, seaweed, whales, seals, and other sea mammals; they also hunted land mammals—bear, caribou, deer, elk. Despite the region's high latitude, the climate is relatively temperate due to the Japanese Current that warms the ocean. It also has a high rainfall that sustains heavy forests, which, in turn, provided an inexhaustible supply of wood for the houses, boats, and other artifacts for which these Indians would become well-known. In fact, one of the distinctive shared cultural elements of the Northwestern peoples is that they were so adept at working wood and other vegetation that they made no pottery.

Because of this hospitable environment, then, the Northwest Coast would support one of the heaviest concentrations of Native Americans in North America—estimated at some 200,000 when the first Europeans made contact late in the sixteenth century. As stated before, it is impossible to pin down all of the modern tribes and groups in precise locations during the millennia before Europeans arrived. But four of the main groups along the northwestern coastline of Alaska and British Columbia were the Tlingit, Haida, Kwakiutl, and Nootka, and although they live outside the territory of the historic American states encompassed by this book, there is every reason to

believe that for thousands of years these peoples had many influential dealings with their relatives to the south.

By the time the first Europeans made contact with this northernmost stretch of the Northwest Coast, these people had devised a distinctive material culture. They excelled at woodcarving, for example, displaying their skill in everything from small boxes and chests to

Right: Skokomish women were famous for weaving soft, flexible baskets. The Skokomish were one of the many Southern Coast Salish who lived along the shores of Washington's Puget Sound.

great totem poles and ceremonial partitions in house-chiefs' apartments. They also carved dugouts of all types from massive tree trunks—great ceremonial canoes of cedar wood were as long as 60 feet. They lived in large multifamily wooden houses, often with elaborately carved central house posts. Even much of their basic clothing was made from cedarbark, but they also used mountain goat wool and dog hair. They often wore decorated conical hats woven from cedar bark or spruce root.

Many of the Northwestern coastal peoples' most notable artifacts were made for various religious and social ceremonies, usually involving dances and music. For their numerous rituals, they made fantastic wooden masks and painted them in striking colors. They also carved intricate wooden rattles, pipes, and ceremonial staffs. The Chilkat Tlingit were especially noted for their so-called blankets, actually robes used for ceremonial occasions and woven from cedar bark and mountain goat wool.

Above: *Beyond the driftwood in the foreground rises Lummi Peak, highest point of the San Juan Islands, located just off the northernmost coast of Washington.*

The story of the ancestors of the Native Americans who have long inhabited the Northwest belongs to the greater story of the peopling of North America. Its basic outline has long been generally agreed upon: during a period of the last Ice Age—roughly 23,000–13,000 BC—when large quantities of the world's waters were locked up in great ice caps and glaciers, people from Asia made their way across the exposed land bridge known as Beringia (so named because it was really the bed of the Bering Sea) and—by at least 12,000 BC—were beginning to move down through corridors in Alaska and Canada. Almost certainly they were relatives of the various peoples liv-

Previous page: *This carving is a detail of a totem pole, typical of several Northwestern tribes. Such figures represent animals or mythological beings with which clans and individuals are often identified.*

Above: An artist has depicted the way the Northwestern people waited silently on the banks of rivers like the Columbia to spear salmon.

houses, totem poles, cedar-bark clothing, basketry, conical hats, and much more. In their social arrangements, too, these people were much alike. On the Olympic Peninsula in the northwest of Washington, for example, lived the Makah Indians, essentially a group of Nootka who had migrated south from Vancouver Island in British Columbia. A subgroup of these Nootka-Makah Indians were the Ozette, who lived alongside the Makah in the Olympic Peninsula; archaeological excavation of an Ozette village has yielded some of the most complete evidence of early Native American life in this region. Apparently, the Makah and Ozette often engaged in warfare against their neighbors to the south, the Quileute.

Somewhat farther south, along the coast bordering the great Columbia River, lived the Chinook. They had highly stratified societies in which the chieftain could help himself to virtually anything he wanted, from food to women. At the same time, high status entailed such obligations as the potlatch feasts. The Chinook of the upper classes kept slaves (who were sometimes killed when the master died so as to serve him in the afterlife). And just across the Columbia River from the Chinook were close relatives, the Clatsop, with whom Lewis and Clark would spend the winter of 1805–6 on their historic expedition.

South of the Clatsop along the Pacific coast of Oregon lived such peoples as the Tillamook, the Upper Umpqua, the Cossans, the Chetco, and the Tututni. Again, most of these peoples shared many of the cultural artifacts and traditions of their more northerly relatives—from basketry and canoes and wooden houses to social elites, slavery, and the potlatch.

power. A potlatch usually involved feasts, speeches, dances, and music, during which ceremonies the host gave away both food and various possessions to the guests. If he was especially determined to show off his wealth, or to challenge a rival to try to outdo him with a potlatch, the host would destroy some valuable possession.

Some of the more extreme elements of these northernmost coastal cultures were not carried down into the future United States. But many of the inhabitants along the coasts of Washington, Oregon, and northern California were probably closely related to the more northerly peoples, and their material culture was much the same—including carved wooden objects, canoes, wooden

Moving downward into northern California, we find many of those same material artifacts, but some cultural elements differed from those of the coastal dwellers to the north. Just south of the Chetco and Tututni of southern Oregon, for instance, were their close relatives, the Tolowa. South of the Tolowa, the Yurok lived near the mouth of the Klamath River. South of the Yurok were the Hupa. These tribes maintained social hierarchies based primarily on the acquisition of wealth, but instead of the potlatch they used this wealth for dowries, fines and indemnities, and gambling. They also had other distinctive cultural elements: leather clothing, ceremonial headdresses made of redheaded-woodpecker scalps, male sweat lodges, and excavated pits in the centers of their wooden houses.

Still closer to San Francisco were the Pomo, whose culture and traditions were considerably different from those of the coast dwellers farther north. Although wealth counted for a great deal in achieving status, chiefs also had to be affiliated with some secret society and participate in councils. Their economy depended heavily on trade and instead of giving away possessions at a potlatch, they gave feasts at which the invited guests were expected to leave payments. Although they depended on the sea for much of their food and also hunted land game, the chief staple of their diet was acorns. They traveled on rafts instead of canoes. And not only were their baskets among the finest of all the Northwest Coast Indians, unlike in most tribes the men also assisted in making them.

Left: This rock—at Chaw Se State Historic Park, California—was used for grinding the nuts and seeds that formed the staple of the local Miwok diet.

Below: This petroglyph is one of several made centuries ago by Indians living along the Columbia River in Washington.

INLAND DWELLERS

The Northwestern peoples who lived well inland from the Pacific Coast were shaped by a different environment and thus developed many different cultural materials and traditions. The territory encompassed by this book includes the vast lands east of the Cascade Range of Washington and Oregon and the section of California roughly north from what is now San Francisco to the borders of Idaho and Nevada. The northern part of this region belongs to the Columbia River basin and as such has a different climate from the coastal stretch to the west. It is semiarid, with summer temperatures approaching those of the deserts and winters that see near-arctic cold. The tribes inhabiting that northern section (in present-day Washington and Oregon) include those known in historic times as the Cayuse, the Coeur d'Alene, Colville, Kalispel, Klikitat, Nez Percé, Okanogan, some of the Salish people, the Sanpoil, the Sinkiuse, the Spokane, Umatilla, Walla Walla, Wishram, and Yakima.

Another group inhabited the more diversified environment of northern California, bordered on the west by the Coast Range, on the east by the Sierra Nevada, and on the north by the Cascades. These included such tribes as the Achumawi, Karuk, Maidu, Miwok, Modoc, Shasta, Wintun, and Yana. A third group inhabited a more challenging environment, the northwestern corner of the Great Basin, which is virtually a desert, extending from southeastern Oregon along the eastern slopes of the Sierra Nevada into northeast California. The tribes who lived in this region include the Northern Paiute and Washo.

Right: Edward Curtis, as part of his epic project documenting North American Indians, photographed this Klamath woman in a dugout canoe cutting rushes in Klamath Lake, Oregon. The rushes were woven to make various domestic items.

Many of these people, of course, were not confined to this relatively narrow territory, but spread eastward into Idaho and even Montana and southward into Nevada. Likewise, tribes at the two extremes shared certain characteristics with their immediate neighbors. The Karuk, for instance, who lived farther west and along the great rivers, depended heavily on the salmon and other fish and made their houses out of cedar planks. Meanwhile, those who lived more to the east, such as the Nez Percé and Cayuse, exhibited much of the culture and ways of their easterly neighbors, the Plains Indians, including, eventually, reliance on the use of the horse for both transport and warfare.

In general, however, the people of this inland region shared certain cultural elements. In the absence of lush coastal forests, they did not develop the coastal

peoples' woodcarving skills but they were masters of basketry, particularly coiled baskets, often woven with ingenious geometric designs. (The Shasta, however, specialized in deerskin containers.) They also made rock paintings, or petroglyphs, for thousands of years. During the winter, many of them lived in semisubterranean pit houses; in summer they often moved into above-ground mat houses of woven plant materials. Some of these tribes used rafts or made their canoes of cedar bark rather than hollowed tree trunks; many used snowshoes, and animal skins were often made into clothing. Some of these groups were seminomadic, moving in search of food supplies—fishing for salmon or other species in season, then tracking deer and other game, and always seeking roots, nuts, seeds, berries, and other edible plants. Acorns, especially, were a staple food.

Overleaf: These colorful painted masks carved from wood are typical of the handiwork of the Northwest Coast Indians. They represent animals and mythological beings and were worn for dances and other ceremonies.

a

b   c

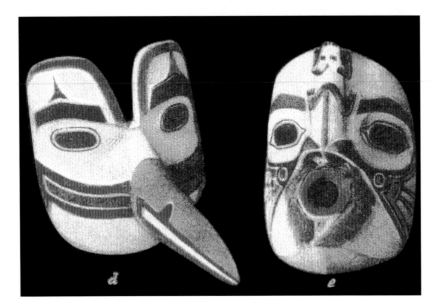

d   e

These, then, were the main tribes of our Northwest: they would be here when the first Europeans arrived and continue to live alongside them. The tribes' names, as noted, might have changed over time, and not all were settled in the same defined territory throughout the period. Certainly, their material cultures showed some changes as the newcomers dispersed among them. Metals and colored beads were only two of several materials that the Native Americans adopted from the traders and explorers. Later, the introduction of the horse and of firearms would have a considerable impact on some of the native peoples. They, in turn, would influence the Europeans. For example, argillite, a fine-grained, dark-grey shale, occurred on the mountainside of Skidegate Inlet in the Queen Charlotte Islands off British Columbia, heartland of the Haida people. Argillite had always been there, and the Indians had evidently used it to make such objects as amulets and lip discs. Not until the early 1800s, however, when Europeans began to show admiration for such carvings, which had a lustrous black finish—did the Haida begin to carve more intricate objects like pipes, flutes, platters, and figurines to satisfy the newcomers' demand. By and large, however, these Northwest peoples maintained their indigenous cultures and societies well into the nineteenth century. Not until explorers and settlers came among them in great numbers did they find their very existence threatened. For the first three centuries or so, the Native Americans and the newcomers coexisted with a certain wary respect for each other's strengths.

EXPLORERS
AND
EARLY SETTLERS

Previous page:
A weathered rock in Washington State's San Juan Islands. Early settlers were intrigued by the wild beauty of the Northwest coast.

When the first Europeans moved onto the eastern lands of the Americas starting in 1492, not only did the residents of the Northwest know nothing of these events, the Northwest was not yet even dreamed of by the Europeans. The story of the subsequent exploration and settlement of that eastern side of the Western Hemisphere is widely regarded as one of the great epics of human history, resonant with such names as Columbus, Cartier, Raleigh, Roanoke, de Soto, Hudson, Captain John Smith, Plymouth, and other icons of the age of exploration. But the fact is that only fifty years after Columbus's landfall, Europeans were making contact with some of the inhabitants of the Northwest, and this story and its aftermath comprise an equally dramatic epic that deserves to be better known.

Though there may have been early sightings by sailors from the Philippines or other parts of Asia, the first known non-natives to arrive were, almost inevitably, the Spanish. Having conquered much of Mexico, Hernándo Cortés sponsored several expeditions that left Mexico's west coast and sailed up into the Sea of Cortés. Then, in 1539, Francisco de Ulloa sailed up along the Pacific coast of Baja California perhaps as far as present-day San Diego (and even that is disputed). Apparently, the first to reach the northwestern shores of the Pacific were the Portuguese explorer Juan Rodrigues Cabrillo and his pilot Bartolomé Ferrelo: sailing north from Mexico in the service of Spain in 1542, they explored the California coastline to Point Reyes, just north of present-day San Francisco. Cabrillo died over the winter, so Ferrelo took command and in 1543 sailed to Cape Mendocino some 350 miles north of San Francisco—perhaps even a few miles north of the future border with Oregon.

Right: *Cortés meeting Montezuma in Mexico City in 1519. The Spanish conquest of Mexico soon led to the exploration of more northerly regions.*

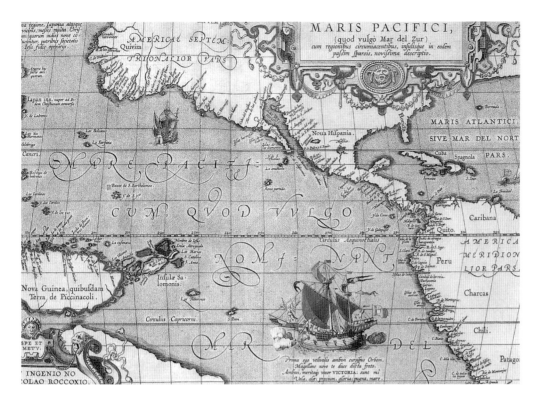

Left: A 1589 map of "Maris Pacifici" by Ortelius demonstrated the extent of European exploration along the Pacific coast. His claim for "Nova Hispania," however, proved overly optimistic.

Thanks to trade between Mexico and the Philippines, Spain had the Pacific coast of the Americas to itself. Although some Spaniards may have occasionally put ashore and made contact with the Native Americans of the Northwest, these groups had little or no impact on each other, and no settlements were made. Before long, however, Spain was not alone. In 1577 Sir Francis Drake, England's celebrated rover and scourge of the Portuguese and Spanish (the latter called him "Francisco Draque," or the "Dragon"), set off on a voyage around the world. Rounding the Strait of Magellan, he headed north in the *Golden Hind* and began seizing Spanish vessels and raiding Spanish settlements along the Pacific coast of South America.

Drake proceeded north, and by May 1579 was somewhere off the coast of northern California. Complaining of worm-eaten planks, rain that he called "an unnatural and congealed frozen substance" and the "most vile, thicke and stinking fogges," he spent more than a month looking for shelter. His point of landfall is a matter of much controversy. Some historians claim he sailed as far north as the 48th parallel, off the Olympic Peninsula. More likely, he got only as far north as what came to be called Drake's Bay—the bay enclosed by the Point Reyes Peninsula, some 25 miles north of present-day San Francisco. Reportedly, wherever he did land, he nailed a brass plate to a post. In 1934 someone claimed to have found this plate at Drake's Bay; but most scholars consider this a modern hoax. Perhaps more significant than the exact point of his landing was Drake's atypical behavior in the first major recorded European contact with natives of the Northwest. There is no evidence of violence, sexual contact, or any form of exploitation on the part of the English. On the contrary, during a June 17–July 23 encounter, probably with the Coast Miwok or Pomo, Drake and his men extolled them for their hospitality, regret-

Opposite:
The coastline near Mendocino, California. One reason explorers were slow to become settlers was the ragged, inhospitable coast and the difficulties it raised for landing craft.

Below: *Drake's Beach north of San Francisco. The famous English explorer is believed to have landed here in 1579.*

ting only that the natives viewed their visitors as gods. The account of Drake's stay was printed in Richard Hakluyt's *The Principall Navigations* (London, 1598). Here we learn that soon after establishing camp on shore, Drake received a group of natives led by a chief the English called a king, "a man of goodly stature and comely personage." Later the English "trevailed up into the Country to their villages, where wee found herdes of Deere by 1000 in a companie, being most large and fat in bodie." The English also reported that "There is no part of earth here to be taken up wherein there is not a reasonable quantitie of gold or silver"

(a claim for which there is no evidence). The account later states that the king and other leaders "made several orations that [Drake] would take their province and kingdome into his hand and become their king, making signes that they would resign unto him their right and title of the whole land and become his subjects." This was probably the Englishmen's biased interpretation of the natives' offers of hospitality, but Drake claimed the whole region for England and named it Nova Albion.

Drake then continued on his voyage around the world, and the Spanish had this region to themselves again. In 1584, Francisco Gali surveyed part of the California coast while sailing his galleon on the return leg of the recently established Spanish trade route between Acapulco, Mexico, and the Philippines. In 1595 Sebastián Rodrigues Cermenho, a Portuguese sailing for the Spanish, sighted land near Trinidad Head, 65 miles south of what is now the California-Oregon border, but he was unable to land until he found Drake's Bay. There he took a launch ashore and proclaimed the site the Bahia de San Francisco. (The San Francisco Bay was not really explored until the late 1700s.) But Cermenho's ship ran aground, and the launch with seventy-some survivors escaped with no chance to map the shoreline.

Despite these setbacks, the new Spanish king, Felipe III, was ready to finance further expeditions. Sebastián Vizcaíno led a Spanish expedition in 1602–1603 that reached the 42nd parallel off Oregon on a voyage tormented by storm and sickness; he left behind a promontory near the California border called Cape San Sebastían. He also recorded a number of friendly encounters with Native Americans and gave them credit for help-

Above: Fort Yukon (1847), a Hudson's Bay Company holding on the Yukon River. The British company, also known as HBC, was so active and widespread that Americans dubbed it "Here Before Christ."

Opposite: An 1800 map commissioned by the Hudson's Bay Company and recorded by A. Arrowsmith. Note the River Oregan, so named by Native Americans and later used in a slightly different form to connote both a territory and a state.

ing to nurse his sick sailors back to health. The natives, Vizcaíno reported, "showed them all the kindness possible." Esteban Lopez reached the 43rd latitude (off southwestern Oregon) in 1603, and Martin de Aguilar explored the coast of northern California and Oregon on a hazardous journey that took his life that same year. The Spanish may have tried unsuccessfully to settle at Monterey Bay in 1607 before being sidetracked by a search for rumored Pacific islands called Rica de Oro and Rica de Plata (rich in gold and silver, respectively). With the prospect of great wealth in the Pacific, the Spanish abandoned their explorations of the northwest Pacific coast.

By the early 1600s, then, both the major European factions were losing interest in the Northwest. It took a Russian connection to bring both nations back to the region. In 1728 Vitus Bering, a Dane sail-

ing for Russia's Tsar Peter the Great, first sighted an island off Alaska. It was not until his second voyage, in 1741, that he sighted the mainland; he went ashore on another Alaskan island, since named for him, where he died of scurvy, but the sea otter pelts his sailors brought back led to occupation of the Aleutian Islands.

Interest began to build, although it was almost another half-century before Europeans' ships were plying the coast. In the meantime, natives told of earlier sightings in the region of Oregon. One party of Europeans leaving a shipwreck is said to have landed at Nehalem Beach along Oregon's northern coast. They remained with the natives until feuds over their attentions to local women resulted in pitched battles that wiped out the intruders, some of whom may have left descendants behind. From a shipwreck on Clatsop Beach in northernmost Oregon emerged two men notable for their long beards and their habit of popping corn. They were made slaves, but were later freed and settled in the Cascades. In 1811 the American-financed Canadian fur trader Gabriele de la Franchère met an old man who claimed to be the son of a Spaniard wrecked in the area. He said all but four men from a Spanish crew had been murdered; the survivors had married native women and disappeared while heading south for Spanish settlements. A Nehalem "Pocahontas" saved and married a red-haired sailor around 1760; the couple lived with a Clatsop chief, and both men later died of an unspecified disease. In 1806 Lewis and Clark discovered a redheaded, freckle-faced Clatsop during their travels.

Perhaps the most famous controversy involves the ten tons of beeswax found at Nehalem Beach. In 1813 explorer Alexander Henry reported that the Clatsops claimed it had been left by Spaniards who were killed by natives, perhaps the men who were killed for exploiting women. According to missionary Daniel Lee, the Hudson's Bay Company bought large amounts of this substance from Indians. In the 1980s, examiners from the United States Geological Survey, Pacific University, and the University of Oregon confirmed that it was beeswax. The large blocks were stamped with initials that Roman Catholics would have recognized from their liturgies, which suggests that the wax was to be used for making candles and images in their missions. The disappearance of the Spanish ship *San Jose*, which left lower California in 1769 with supplies intended for the San Diego Mission, might explain the mystery.

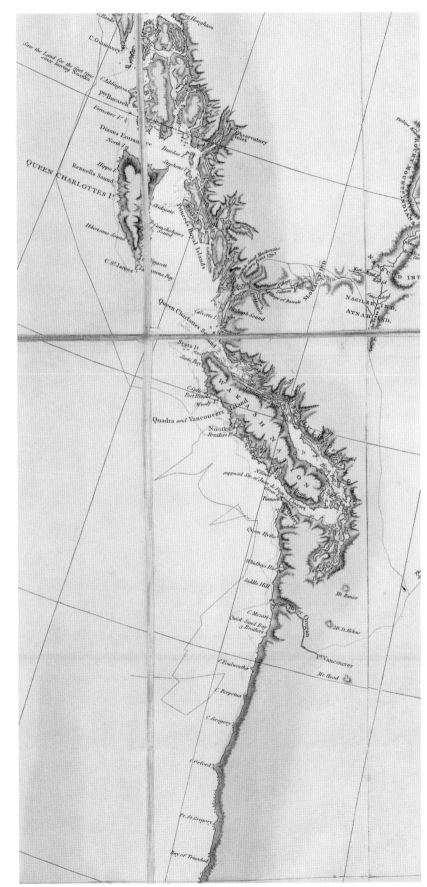

Verified encounters were every bit as mysterious and often disastrous. Many involved the Columbia River that separates Washington and Oregon. In 1775 the Spaniard Bruno Hecata, after landing at Port Grenville, Washington, anchored between the shores of the river, which were six miles apart, and realized that he had found "the mouth of some great river, or some passage to another sea." (This first recorded sighting of the Columbia River by a European would not be recognized until much later.) Unfortunately, Hecata thought that Oregon's Clatsop Plains were an island and decided he could enter the river elsewhere. In a small boat with a crew of fourteen, he headed seaward and failed to make his way back. In his honor the Spanish named the bay Hecata's Inlet. In 1788 Captain John Meares, a Briton sailing with Portuguese papers, also found the bay, but saw what appeared to be an impassable series of breakers. His log recorded that "We can now with safety assert that no such river as that of the St. Roc exists, as laid down in the Spanish

Right: Fort Ross, which was established in present-day Washington State by Russia in 1812. The impetus of early settlement was trapping, first of sea otter, then of beaver.

Opposite: Oregon's Mount Hood, of volcanic origin, and the Hood River Valley. The state's highest mountain at 11,235 feet, Mount Hood is also called Wy'east, for a mythical Native American warrior who threw rocks and fire into the air.

charters…We now reached the opposite side of the bay, where disappointment continued to accompany us; and, being almost certain that there we should obtain no place of shelter for the ship, we bore up for a distant headland, keeping our course within two miles of the shore." Meares named what he assumed was only a bay Deception Bay and the headland Cape Disappointment, unaware how badly he had been deceived by the turbulent estuary. He, too, had found the mouth of the Columbia, the West's greatest river.

Others had more success. Juan Perez discovered the Nootka Sound, British Columbia, in 1774. Juan Francisco de la Bodega y Quadra sailed up along the Oregon coast, and later to the 58th parallel, in 1775, and landed in Alaska. In 1776 the Spanish constructed a military base and mission on the San Francisco peninsula; the former, ill-defended, became a "liberty stop" for ships, while

the latter became the core of a settlement. In 1778, on his fateful third voyage, Captain James Cook explored coastal Oregon, Washington, and British Columbia and sighted Alaska. He sailed on to his death in the Sandwich Islands (Hawaii), but not before discovering furs that cost a few cents in the Pacific Northwest and could be sold for great sums in Guangdong, China. The lure of the sea otter drew several new participants to the Pacific Northwest.

Among these were some nascent Americans. In 1783 one Captain John Ledyard of Hartford, Connecticut, a corporal on Cook's flagship, published an account of Cook's voyage with the intention of getting merchants to sponsor his own expedition. Ledyard failed, but a Boston company dispatched two ships in 1787: the 220-ton *Columbia* under John Kendrick and the 90-ton *Lady Washington* under Robert Gray.

Below: An engraving from James Cook's A Voyage to the Pacific Ocean *called "A View of the Habitations in Nootka Sound." Located in today's British Columbia, the sound was visited by sailors from several different countries.*

Arriving at Nootka Sound in 1788, they found British captains who had antagonized both the native people and the Spanish. Once the British left, Gray and Kendrick exchanged ships and traded harmoniously with the indigenous peoples. When the star-crossed British navigators returned, their ships were seized by the Spaniard Bodega y Quadra in a dispute over Canada's Nootka Sound. The Spanish felt that the Americans were interested in trading rather than territory and left them alone.

Gray eventually sailed to China, becoming the first American to circumnavigate the world. For his part, Kendrick reached the Strait of Juan de Fuca and sailed around Vancouver Island. The discovery of this strait, which stretches between Vancouver Island and Washington's Olympic Peninsula, is usually attributed to Charles William Barkley, who sailed his English fur-trading vessel into its waters in 1787. But its unusual name derives from the pseudonym of a Greek seafarer, Apostolos Valerianos, who claimed to have discovered such a strait in 1592 while serving as the pilot for an expedition sponsored by the Spanish viceroy in Mexico.

If anything, Captain Gray's second voyage, starting in 1791, was even more significant. His *Columbia* met amicably with the British captain George Vancouver and his ship *Discovery*. Still seeking the Northwest Passage, Vancouver had headed north to the Strait of Juan de Fuca, the Gulf of Georgia, and to Vancouver Island, mapping the area and leaving behind such names as Mount Rainier and Puget Sound. To the south, Gray risked challenging the breakers on May 11, 1792, and found the continent's second longest river, which Vancouver had ignored, and named it the Columbia

in a spirit of acquisition. Then he made his way upriver a short distance in search of furs and returned with beaver pelts. Five months later, Britain's William R. Broughton, who knew of Gray's exploits, sailed about 100 miles up the newly discovered Mount Hood River in the Cascade Range, and claimed the region for England on grounds that "the subjects of no other civilized nation or state had entered this river before." Because the natives called the river the Oregan, or Ouregon, the area between the Rockies and Pacific, and the vaguer border of Spanish possessions to the south and British and Russian land to the north, would soon become known in English as the Oregon country or territory.

Spain had foresworn its claims to a monopoly on trade and settlement north of San Francisco when it resolved its differences with England in the Nootka Convention of 1790. The United States and England were quick to launch overland expeditions to establish claims to this territory. In 1792 the Northwest Company of British fur-trading fame commissioned a Scotsman, Alexander Mackenzie, to explore the Northwest, and he became the first European to traverse the continent, coming across the Rocky Mountains to reach the Pacific coast of British Columbia. As early as 1796, the first American trading ship, the *Otter*, appeared along the northern California coast. But it was another seven years before President Jefferson made the decision that irrevocably changed the region's history.

In 1803 Jefferson ordered Meriwether Lewis and William Clark to lead an expedition to explore the vast territory west of the Mississippi all the way to the Pacific. Contrary to popular belief,

Overleaf: A rocky inlet at Cape Flattery, on the northwest end of Washington's Olympic Peninsula. It faces the famous Strait of Juan de Fuca and British Columbia.

Below: A Charles Russell painting depicts the Lewis and Clark expedition in a Mandan village. Thanks in part to their Shoshone interpreter Sacajawea, the travelers were well treated by Native Americans during their two-year (1804–06) trek.

Jefferson was not originally motivated by a desire to explore the Louisiana Purchase, because that transaction was not complete at the time: he was far more concerned about staking a claim to the remote Northwest and the valuable fur trade before the British took over. Setting off from St. Louis in May 1804, the party made its way up the Missouri River and across the Rocky Mountains. Reduced in rations at times to eating dog and horsemeat and spoiled elk, the Lewis and Clark expedition eventually reached the Columbia River, and finally, the coast. On November 17, 1805, they built Fort Clatsop, near present-day Astoria, Oregon, where they spent a miserable winter marked by almost constant rain. By the time they returned to St. Louis on September 23, 1806, they had been given up for dead. Their epic journey established a permanent U.S. presence in the Northwest.

Reading of the discoveries of Lewis and Clark, many Americans yearned to go west, but for years to come, the major activity in the Northwest was not settlement, but a heated fur-trading rivalry between the United States and Great Britain. The first British fur-trading operations in the territory were those of the North West Company whose chief man on the scene was David Thompson. He had originally been apprenticed to the Hudson's Bay Company (HBC), founded in 1670 and long the dominant force in the fur trade within eastern Canada. Thompson served as a clerk, hunter, trader, astronomer, and surveyor. In 1797 he signed on with the better-paying North West Company, and ten years later he crossed the Continental Divide and built Kootenai House, a trading post in eastern British Columbia.

In 1811 Thompson moved down the Columbia River from Kettle Falls in eastern Washington to the Pacific, getting support from hundreds of natives along the way. Thompson hoped to claim the Northwest region for England, but when he arrived at the mouth of the Columbia, a group of Americans was already building a trading outpost. They had sailed there from New York City, sent by the Pacific Fur Company, which was owned by John Jacob Astor, a German who had emigrated to New York in 1784 and prospered greatly in the fur trade. The new Fort Astoria (which was not far from the Fort Clatsop of Lewis and Clark) was the first permanent settlement founded by Americans along the Pacific coast.

Now competition between the two nations' fur traders became intense. The

British (1810) built a fort in Spokane, Washington, the Americans (1811) constructed the first permanent settlement in central Washington, Fort Okanogan. And the trade was not restricted to these contenders: in 1812, the Russians built Fort Ross in northern California. (This was one of the reasons that President James Monroe pronounced his 1823 "doctrine" that sovereign states in North and South America were closed to European colonization.)

Fearing a violent takeover during the War of 1812, Astor's company abandoned Fort Astoria in 1813 to the North West Company, which then renamed it Fort George. Even though the Treaty of Ghent ending the war reassigned the place to the United States, Astor sold it back to the British in 1814. In 1821 the Hudson's Bay Company bought up the North West Company and so acquired Fort George. (By this time the Hudson's Bay Company owned so many trading posts in the Northwest that Americans said HBC stood for "Here before Christ.")

In 1824 relations between the British and Americans in the region would begin to change with the assignment of Dr. John McLoughlin to build and head the Hudson's Bay Company's chief outpost in the region, Fort Vancouver (at present-day Vancouver, Washington). Known as the "White-headed Eagle," he was so obsessed with keeping Americans from his prime beaver country that he had trapper Peter Skene Ogden capture every animal he could find over a six-year period. However, he was also generous with Americans and natives alike. By this time, a new message was going out from the Northwest: settlers are wanted. But many hardships were still to come for all concerned.

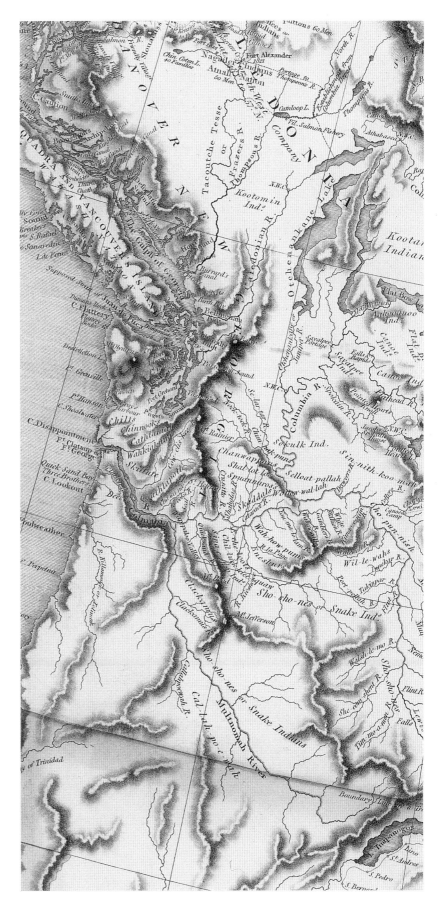

Right: *The Fort Clatsop National Memorial, with a replica of a log fort built by Lewis and Clark in 1805.*

Below: *Sand dunes and Captain's Rock near the Columbia River in eastern Washington. Encountering Walla Walla Indians, Lewis and Clark camped here in the fall of 1805. Fort Nez Percé (later renamed Fort Walla Walla) was established by British fur traders in the 1820s.*

FORGING
THEIR
DESTINIES

Above: *The first log cabin built in Yosemite Valley, circa 1895.*

Previous page: *An 1880s cannon outside the Mono County Courthouse in Bridgeport, California. Originally called Big Meadows, the town was settled by 1850s farmers and cattlemen including George (By) Day and Napoleon Bonaparte Hunewill.*

When they signed an 1818 codicil to the Treaty of Ghent that had ended the war of 1812, the United States and Great Britain agreed to joint occupancy of the Oregon Territory. Both sides were to be allowed to develop the region without setting up governments. But exactly what was the Oregon Territory? The more the Hudson's Bay Company expanded its fur-trading interests, the larger the territory became. When the company acquired the rival North West Company in 1821, the region enlarged to the size of Washington and Idaho, as well as Oregon and a sizable chunk of Canada.

The Oregon Territory had become an Anglo-American region in 1819 when the United States and Spain signed the Adams-Onis Treaty, which established the Oregon-California boundary at latitude 42° north—essentially the modern border between the states. After Mexico won its independence from Spain in 1821, its government claimed all of California. By 1827 Russia had claimed only the territory north of 54° 40', and a small number of Russian nationals remained in the Oregon Territory until the 1840s.

What ultimately tipped the area south of the 49th parallel—the present northwest border between Canada and the United States, except Vancouver Island— in favor of the United States was a heavy influx of settlers and missionaries. It mattered not whether they were explicitly religious: many of those who arrived in Oregon were looking for a purer life than they had experienced back East. By the mid-1800s, there was said to be a fork in the Oregon Trail where travelers had to decide whether to head for California or Oregon. The southerly sign, supposedly marked by quartz, could have read "Beware all ye who enter here," so rabid was the gold fever. The northerly sign, said to read only, "To Oregon," might have said, "Eden ahead."

Of course, the Oregon Territory was not really heavenly, but newcomers did have visions before their eyes. In 1817 a Bostonian named Hall Jackson Kelley read *The Journals of Lewis and Clark* and promptly decided that "the word came expressly to me to go and labor in the field of philanthropic enterprise and promote the propagation of Christianity in the dark and cruel places about the shores of the Pacific."

After failing at several businesses, in 1829 Kelley founded the American Society for Encouraging the Settlement of the Oregon Territory, which was incorporated by the Massachusetts legislature. Plagiarizing, inventing, and using some published journals, Kelley published an 1831 report on the "New Eden" he had never visited. Getting there, however, was not so easy. Taking some settlers by the roundabout sea-land route to the Columbia River in 1832, he was robbed in New Orleans by his own party, whom he immediately dismissed; stripped of his property by Mexican customs officials; stricken with malaria; jailed for an entire winter by the Hudson's Bay Company's John McLoughlin when he finally reached Fort Vancouver (1834) in the company of hunters, trappers, and "marauders"; and shipped off to Hawaii. Drifting into madness, libeling his rivals, Kelley published an 1839 memoir that somehow made Oregon more enticing still.

Meanwhile, many missionaries were intrigued by the account of "The Four Wise Men from the West"—Nez Percé Indians who reached St. Louis in 1832 to discuss the Bible with William Clark. Two of them died, and the others headed west to tell their tribe how disappointed they were with the white man's book and ungodly St. Louis. Evangelicals saw them and other Native Americans as lost souls and set out to convert them.

__Below:__ Pioneer Village in Cashmere, Washington. Built in 1873 at the state's geographical center, Cashmere got its current name when Judge James H. Chase compared its beauty to the Vale of Kashmir in the northwestern Indian Subcontinent.

Above: *A Conestoga wagon. Laboring across the Oregon Trail, these vehicles, covered by canvas tops, took settlers from the Midwest to the Northwest.*

Opposite, above:
A statue of James W. Marshall, who discovered gold at Sutter's Mill. Note the Bear Flag accompanying Old Glory.

Opposite, below:
A wagon at the Donner Memorial near Truckee, California. In 1846–7, the ill-fated Donner Party lost half of its members to starvation, exposure, and cannibalism.

The rich, green land inspired migration for religious and secular reasons alike. Reaching Oregon's Grande Ronde Valley with a 110-man, twenty-wagon trading expedition in 1833, the French-born captain Benjamin Bonneville proclaimed: "Its sheltered situation, embosomed in mountains, renders it good pasturing ground in the winter time; when the elk come down to it in great numbers, driven out of the mountains by the snow. The Indians then resort to it to hunt. They likewise come to it in the summer to dig the camas root, of which it produces immense qualities. When the plant is in blossom, the whole valley is tinted by its blue flowers, and looks like the ocean when overcast by a cloud."

A Kelley supporter, Nathanial Wyeth, built Fort Hall on Idaho's Snake River in 1834. Accompanying him on his expedition were the first missionaries to reach the Northwest, Methodists Jason Lee and his nephew Daniel, founders of an 1835 mission station and school

10 miles from Salem, Oregon, that became Willamette University. That same year more missionaries arrived from the East, the most promising being Marcus Whitman. After a visit back home, he returned in 1836 and settled in Waiilatpu, Washington, near the confluence of the Columbia and Walla Walla Rivers. With him this time was Henry Harmon Spalding, who established a community near Lewiston, in Idaho. Whitman's and Spalding's wives—respectively named Narcissa and Eliza—were the first non-native women to cross the Continental Divide. Father Francis J. Blanchette reached St. Paul, Oregon, in 1838 to minister to Roman Catholics: he also confused Indians about the nature of the Christian religion. Despite little success in converting French Canadians and natives, Whitman and Jason Lee subsequently returned East to ask for governmental aid and protection. In 1843 the first significant wagon train, a "great migration" of 900 souls, arrived, followed by another 1,200 in 1844.

Oregonians like to brag that their forebears were a superior breed. Well, they were certainly courageous, and they were well equipped—at least when they started their journeys west. They embarked on the two-thousand-mile Oregon Trail in canvas-covered wagons, with cattle and livestock hitched behind, and enough food and provisions to last six months. By the time they had set off from Independence, Missouri, followed the North Platte River to the South Pass in Wyoming, traversed the Snake River Plain in Idaho, and crossed the Blue Mountains to the Columbia River at the Dalles, virtually everything might be gone. And the toughest part of their journey lay ahead.

Their choices: raft all their supplies through the rapids at the Columbia River Gorge, or climb up Mount Hood and down the treacherous Barlow Trail to the Willamette Valley, often lowering their wagons by rope. Those who reached the final destination, Oregon City, were often bereft of everything, including family members, and had to rely on the kindness of strangers to survive their first winter. The creation of a second, more southerly route, known as the Applegate Trail, eased the trip, but in 1849 only 8,779 people resided in all of Oregon (excluding Native Americans).

Oddly, a mass exodus to California because of the gold rush of 1849 proved to be Oregon's very salvation. Miners returned with $2 million in gold, the legislature minted standardized coins, and Oregonians began shipping their produce and lumber to California.

California's new settlers experienced their own share of new challenges. Shipwrecked at the Columbia River in 1841, mineral expert James Dwight Dana and his party journeyed by horseback to San Francisco by following the Sacramento River and stayed with the Swiss landowner John A. Sutter (of whom more later). That same year the Bidwell-Bartelson party arrived in Sacramento as the state's first organized American settlers.

Of course, not every journey went smoothly, or even reached its destination. In October 1846 the Donner Party, a group of eighty-nine immigrants from Springfield, Illinois, led by brothers Jacob and George Donner, was directed away from the usual California trail by organizer Lansford W. Hastings, and became snowbound in the High Sierra, near the border of Nevada and California. Ten

Above: An old firehouse from the gold-rush era in Fiddletown, California. Founded by Missourians in 1849, Fiddletown got its name when an elder complained that the town's young men were "always fiddling."

men, including the two native guides, and five women—the "Forlorn Hope," as they came to be called—set off for help. When four died, the survivors, weeping, ate their flesh. Two more died, and the survivors later shot and ate the two guides. On January 10, 1847, the seven remaining stragglers found a native village. The first rescue party reached the snowed-in emigrants, some of whom had also resorted to cannibalism, on February 19, 1847. In all, only forty-five of the eighty-nine travelers survived the ordeal.

The California they found was transforming rapidly. Because President James K. Polk had run on a platform of annexing California, invasion was inevitable. Leading an expedition into the Mexican-owned territory, John C. Frémont raised a flag at Hawke's Peak north of Monterey in March 1846. On June 14, shortly after the United States declared war on Mexico, a band of thirty-one men captured the northern-California capital of Sonoma and unfurled a flag bearing a red star and a grizzly bear, with the words "California Republic" below them. Around the same time, United States marines and sailors led by Captain John B. Montgomery anchored at Yerba Buena in San Francisco Bay, splashed ashore, and planted an American flag. The following year the village was renamed San Francisco, thus keeping alive the name of the original Spanish mission church on the site.

The Bear Flag Republic lasted only until July 7, 1846, when Commodore John D. Sloat captured Monterey and raised the American flag as a symbol of United States control over all California. When the Treaty of Guadalupe Hidalgo ended the war with Mexico on January 15, 1848, the United States acquired land from Texas to the Pacific and from Mexico up to Oregon. California's large Mexican population had to adjust to new governors.

But all this was to change in ways unforeseen when, on January 24, foreman James W. Marshall discovered gold at John Sutter's mill near Coloma. It was not the first gold strike in California, but it quickly became the most renowned. When President Polk announced it in his December message to Congress, everyone from Easterners to Europeans seemed to be California-bound. At the time there were some 7,300 Anglos and Mexicans in California. Thanks to the emigrating "forty-niners," the population had swelled beyond the 60,000 needed for statehood within a year.

Even then, events in California could make waves elsewhere. The prospect of its becoming a state fired up debate over slavery in the territories, an issue leading to the Civil War. In an 1849 constitutional convention, the Californians banned slavery, not in principle, but because they feared blacks would compete with whites in the mines. Skipping territorial status, Congress admitted California to the Union as a free state in the Compromise of 1850.

The subsequent history of northern California is as varied as the state itself. On one level, it was a free-for-all. When minerals ran low, companies took over

Left: An old jail in Columbia State Historical Park, California.

Below: A wagon in the virtually abandoned gold-rush town of Hornitos, California. Originally a Mexican community, Hornitos grew to 15,000 people during the gold rush and was known for both the infamous bandit Joaquin Murieta and the Ghirardelli chocolate store, whose owner prospered in San Francisco.

Right: The Mark Twain statue in Utica Park, Angels Camp, California. Twain (Samuel Clemens) was one of many writers who settled in the San Francisco area after the Civil War.

Below: The John Muir Historical Site (1882) located in Martinez, California, home to the famous naturalist.

mines and the cost of food and supplies outstripped wages. Bitter men formed vigilante committees in San Francisco. Myriad injustices followed, including the murder of a United States marshal and a newspaper editor, Native Americans were murdered or separated from their families, Mexicans were deprived of their lands, and Chinese immigrants given only abandoned mining claims to work.

A new, far more civilized, northern California was also emerging. After the Civil War ended in 1865 without really affecting the Northwest, San Francisco became a haven for writers like Mark Twain (Samuel Langhorne Clemens)

and Bret Harte. California's first millionaire, one Samuel Brannan, was an excommunicated Mormon, a swindler, and a vigilante who opened a spa in Calistoga in 1866. The Transcendentalist writer, naturalist, and Sierra Club founder John Muir, who called nature a "window opening into heaven, a mirror reflecting the Creator," began working to save the redwoods in 1867. And the plant breeder and horticulturist Luther Burbank, who developed many new strains of fruits, vegetables, and plants, settled in Santa Rosa to begin his botanical experiments in 1875.

Ever conscious of their appearance to sophisticated Easterners, Californians even began building trophy homes: among them were John Bidwell's stylish Italianate house for his wife in Chico; the ornate Carson mansion in Eureka; and the McHenry mansion in Modesto. California was more firmly connected to the East when the Central Pacific Railroad joined up with an Eastern counterpart at Promontory Point, Utah, in 1869. The first continental railroad was achieved thanks to the rare co-operation between ethnic groups: Chinese workers laying track from the west and Irish workers from the east.

The Oregon Territory was also headed for statehood. Ironically, the British originally had a leg up in this. John McLoughlin, chief factor of the Hudson's Bay Company (HBC) from 1824 until 1845, controlled an area larger than England for two decades. He had no legal authority over Americans, but his point of leverage was strategically located at Fort Vancouver on the Columbia. When Nathanial Wyeth sold the American Fort Hall to the Hudson's Bay Company in 1834, McLoughlin seemed to have secured both the fur trade and the interior of the Oregon Territory for England.

That was the year, however, that the first American missionaries arrived. Instead of opposing them, McLoughlin used his expertise in agriculture and cattle-ranching to help them settle in the Willamette Valley, south of the Columbia, and even financed their efforts. He wanted the settlers to depend on Fort Vancouver, but he also had humanitarian concerns. Eventually, he hoped, the Columbia would separate British and U.S. territory in North America, but the successful American settlement of the interior brought more and more wagon trains into the territory.

The 1840s were the final straw. First, McLoughlin quarreled with his British superiors, who were considering moving operations north. Then "the great migration," composed largely of emigrants from the Midwest, convinced the British that it was fruitless to hang onto the territory. Partly because he was already involved in

the Mexican War, President Polk ignored some settlers' belligerent demands of "54–40 or fight" and settled—with the Oregon Treaty of 1846—for 49° minus Vancouver Island as the formal border between the two countries.

Two potential states were taking shape. In more populous Oregon, a debate over annexation and statehood had been raging for some time. The varied population included John McLoughlin, his fellow Roman Catholics from French Canada, and other British subjects. On the American side were Methodists, retired trappers, and other mountain men, many of them preaching the philosophy of "manifest destiny"—the conviction that

Below: *The opulent Carson Mansion in Eureka, California. Built by the lumber baron William Carson, it gave the young state the appearance of a long history.*

Right: *A nineteenth-century photograph of Main Street in a town in Lane County, Oregon, named for the territory's first governor. Note "Furniture and Undertaking" were in the same building as the hospital.*

Opposite and below: *Wagons and buildings in Shaniko, Oregon, which got its name from an early settler, August Sherneckau.*

Above: *An old English camp at Washington's San Juan Historic Park, site of the "Pig War." In 1859 an American settler killed a pig wandering from an English camp into his garden, setting off a thirteen-year dispute over the border between Canada and the United States. Under the 1871 Treaty of Washington, Emperor Wilhelm I of Germany decided in favor of the United States.*

Americans had a semi-divine mission to expand their territory as far as possible. When Congress refused to send in troops, however, the settlers were on their own.

In 1843 voters from the 700 residents of Oregon's Willamette Valley, more or less equally divided among British, Canadians, and Americans, gathered at Champoeg. In an up-and-down vote, a small majority decided to set up a provisional government independent of the HBC—in effect, signing up with the United States. A few votes the other way, and the former Oregon Territory might be British today. After President Polk signed the Oregon Treaty of 1846, John McLoughlin went on to accept American citizenship and eventually became referred to as "The Father of Oregon."

Oregon Territory soon became two territories. After the region gained territorial status in 1848 (Abraham Lincoln declined an offer to serve as governor), Congress passed the Oregon Donation Land Law (1850), giving single men 320 acres and many married couples 640 acres, regardless of whether natives or Britons happened to own the property in question. In 1853 Congress established the Washington Territory, including parts of Idaho and Montana, north of the Columbia River and installed Indian agent and surveyor Isaac Ingalls Stevens as governor. The creation of the Idaho Territory (in 1863) and the Montana Territory (1864) completed Washington State's present borders.

Despite their affiliation with the United States, Oregon voters rejected the idea of a constitutional convention three times, preferring autonomous rule. The Supreme Court's 1857 Dred Scott Decision changed everything. The court ruled that only a sovereign state, not a territory, could decide whether or not to allow slavery. In thinking eerily similar to that prevailing in California, Oregonians didn't object to slavery as much as they did to Native Americans, Chinese, blacks, or anyone else visibly different from themselves. In writing their constitution that year, they banned both slavery and free African Americans, who were literally whipped within an inch of their lives until they left. In this anomalous condition Oregon became the thirty-third state, with Salem as its capital, in 1859.

Oddly, Oregon reversed itself by ratifying the Fourteenth Amendment, which gave the rights of citizenship to former slaves, and progressive Republicans replaced pro-slavery Democrats in many positions of power. One supporter of minority rights, journalist/railroad promoter Henry Villard, installed exhibits on the Northwest at the 1876 Centennial in Philadelphia, which encouraged eighteen thousand people to relocate to Oregon the next year. When he helped make Portland a hub for railroad and steamship commerce, a local editor called the city the "metropolis of the region."

Overwhelmed by Indian wars and an exodus for gold fields from California to British Columbia, Washington developed less rapidly than Oregon. Such population as it had was almost entirely west of the Cascade Mountains. In November 1852, the schooner *Exact* disgorged a few European Americans into a pathetic sandpit where West Seattle is located today. They named the area "New York, Alki," which in local argot meant "New York, someday."

Only a few months later, most of them abandoned Alki to accept an offer from Dr. David Maynard of a site, on Puget Sound, five miles north. They settled in

Left: *The city hall and fire department in Index, Washington. The town is located in the midst of the Cascade Mountains, which extend from Canada to northern California.*

Seattle, named for Chief Seathl of the Duwamish people. In addition to the bay site, endless rains had produced a huge green forest—hence, the nickname "Emerald City"—on a bluff behind the village. Henry M. Yesler built a mill that provided instant employment. Logs were skidded down a chute known as a "skid road." When the downtown evolved into a haven for derelicts, houses of prostitution, and other seedy ventures, the term "skid row" was coined to describe the deteriorated section of a city.

As late as 1860, there were about ten men to every woman in the territory. Asa S. Mercer, the president of Territorial University, vowed to right this wrong. Heading east to Massachusetts, he organized the emigration of young women by advertising employment as schoolteachers and music instructors. Eleven young women—called "Mercer Girls"—arrived to a public reception in Seattle in 1864. The *Seattle Gazette* announced, in purple prose, that: "It is to the efforts of Mr. Mercer, joined with the wishes of the darlings themselves, that the eleven accomplished and beautiful young ladies whose arrival was lately announced have been added to our population….Mr. Mercer is the Union candidate for joint councilman of King and Kitsap counties, and all bachelors, young and old, may on election day have an opportunity of expressing, through the ballot box, their appreciation of his devotion to the cause of Union, matrimonial as well as national." He won by a great majority, the women were employed and married, and two years later Mercer brought ninety-five more emigrants—many of them married men with families—on a ship from New York. Four of the women married during the voyage, including one to Mercer.

However, life was not entirely harmonious in the territory. By failing to import more women, Mercer was eventually isolated and probably sleepless in Seattle. Residents resented territorial governor Stevens for, among other things, suspending civil laws, and fought with Tacoma when that city was chosen as the terminus of the Northern Pacific continental railroad (Portland, Oregon, having already been serving in this capacity). Fighting tooth and nail, Seattleites prevented Mount Rainier from being renamed Mount Tacoma. (The city's nonconforming and independent spirit was not born yesterday.)

The territory's economy picked up during the 1880s. The Northern Pacific connection of 1883 encouraged commerce and settlers, who claimed huge homesteads. Culture was becoming established as well. Port Townsend and Bellingham, with their fine Victorian homes, were settled. George Washington Bush, an African American who fled Oregon's racism, founded Centralia,

Above: Mount Rainier, whose name was hotly contested between residents of Seattle and Portland, became a National Park in 1899. Paradise Inn is one of the park's two historic lodges.

Opposite: The 1914 Wilson Lighthouse, an important beacon at the entrance to Puget Sound at Fort Worden, Port Townsend, Washington. Built in 1902 to guard Puget Sound cities and the Bremerton Naval Yard, the fort was named after Admiral John L. Worthern, commander of the U.S. vessel Monitor, of Civil War fame.

Below: A listing old house in Sierra City, California, is lucky to be standing at all. Sierra City was buried by an avalanche in 1853, but a new settlement was built five years later in a county where some 2 million ounces of gold have been found.

Washington, and thrived there. The state's population increased by 95,000 between 1887 and 1889. When railroad builder James J. Hill made Seattle a terminus for the Great Pacific and cultivated trade with Japan for the Emerald City in 1889, Washington D.C. made Washington Territory the forty-second state, with Olympia as its capital.

Like a rock-'em, sock-'em football game, Washington's boom went bust and then boom again. The Panic of 1893 wiped out everything—mines, mills, and homesteads. But four years later, gold was discovered in the Yukon, and virtually all Alaskan travelers had to pass through Washington. Servicing the avid gold-seekers, western Washington grew rapidly, and eastern Washington happily shipped in produce. A period of progressivism opened the twentieth century, with reform legislation passed on every issue from pure food and drugs to women's suffrage. Washingtonians toasted the decade by staging the Alaska-Yukon-Pacific Exposition of 1909.

THE
INDIAN WARS

Previous page:
Mossbrae Falls on
California's Mount
Shasta. Its sacred
healing waters held
spiritual significance
for Modoc, Shasta,
and other local tribes.

The stories of the nineteenth-century wars between the newcomers and Native Americans in the Northwest are not as well known to most Americans as are those in several other regions of the United States. But the fact is that from the first contacts between old and new peoples in these lands, there were overt hostilities. Perhaps one reason they are not so well known is that the Northwestern Indian wars rarely involved such dramatic incidents as great battles, massive outright land grabs, or overtly broken treaties. To be sure, settlers and traders did encroach on native lands, bringing with them collateral demands for rights of way, hunting grounds, farmland, ranchland, and, eventually, mineral rights. But as often as not, individual conflicts were touched off by more subtle factors introduced by the newcomers: disease, suspicion, arrogance, and ignorance.

The first explorers and traders who put into harbors along the Northwest coast, as we have seen, often engaged in skirmishes with the Native Americans,

and there were killings by both sides. But as it happened, the first American incursion among the Northwestern peoples did not result in any fatalities: this was the Lewis and Clark expedition, which, as mentioned, wintered over at Fort Clatsop near the mouth of the Columbia River in 1805–6. However, when John Jacob Astor's Pacific Fur Company established the Oregon trading post of Astoria in 1811, several workers were killed by the local Chinook.

In 1813 Astor's ship *Tonquin* sailed up the Columbia River and encountered other Chinook at Baker's Bay. In part because the American captain, Jonathan Thorn, antagonized them with what historian George W. Fuller called "insulting and violent conduct," the natives decided to attack. Purportedly vowing to leave insults behind and do some trading, they came on board. One of Astor's partners, Alexander Mackay, warned Thorn to be careful, but the imperious captain refused to drop nets and limit the number of visitors. When the Chinook swarmed on board, out-

Right: William Clark
and Meriwether Lewis.
Their expedition to
the Northwest involved
contact with some fifty
tribes and only one
Indian death. Clark,
later superintendent of
Indian affairs for the
Louisiana Territory, was
especially known for
considerate treatment
of Native Americans.

Left: Colonel Frank Wheaton (standing, center) and officers and family members at Washington's Fort Walla Walla in 1874. Previously successful in fighting Confederates and Cheyenne, Wheaton took a bad beating from the Modoc in the Battle of the Stronghold (1873).

numbering the unarmed sailors, Thorn ordered the visitors to leave and the ship to sail. With weapons concealed beneath their furs, the boarding party slaughtered almost everyone on board and even ran down and killed several escapees. In all, seventeen Americans and twelve Hawaiian Islanders perished. At some point, the ship blew up, killing some 200 natives. This story of the *Tonquin* massacre was told by a single eyewitness, an Indian named Kasiascall, and may not be completely accurate.

After this incident, Kasiascall and fellow natives reportedly intended to attack Fort Astoria, but did not follow through because they believed mistakenly that their plan had been discovered. Another of Astor's expeditions, this one led by John Reed, lost all nine men to disease, injury, and Snake Indian attacks on Washington's Snake River. In all, some sixty members of the Astor enterprise lost their lives—not all to hostilities—but the fort did establish American claims to the region.

The next provocateur/victim was Marcus Whitman, the physician and Presbyterian missionary who established the mission in Waiilatpu, near the present-day Walla Walla, Washington, in 1836. From the beginning, however sincere his faith, his attitude was arrogant. He believed that the natives could be saved only by a "superior" culture, that is, the Christian culture of Europe as transposed to the Americas.

Left: John J. Astor, whose fur traders established a fort in Astoria, Oregon, and a major U.S. claim to the Northwest region. Unfortunately, when they strayed from the stockade, his men were easy prey for resentful Native Americans, and they sold the fort to the British in 1813.

Right: Fort Clatsop in Astoria, Oregon. Named for the local Clatsop Indians, it was home for the Lewis and Clark expedition in the winter of 1805–6. What we see today is a historically accurate reconstruction.

After six unsuccessful years, the American Board of Commissioners for Foreign Missions told Whitman and his colleague Henry Harmon Spalding to abandon their missions. Whitman completed a hazardous journey East, convinced the board to relent, and returned to the Oregon Territory with the "great migration" of 1843, discovering to his horror that his wife, Narcissa, had been attacked in their home by a native and removed to a nearby fort for safety. Subsequently the Whitman mission became a way station and hospital for immigrants to the region.

Whitman failed to convert the local Cayuse, Umatilla, and Walla Walla to his religion or culture. Instead, they caught the newcomers' diseases. During one especially severe outbreak of measles that killed almost half the Cayuse in 1846–7, Whitman gave them medication despite a warning that they might turn on unsuccessful medicine men. When they saw that few Americans were sick, the Cayuse concluded that Whitman had given good medicine to his people and

bad medicine to theirs. They also felt, not unnaturally, that the settlers had given them measles, although it may also have been transported from California by natives who had fought alongside Americans in the Mexican War.

Sickness was perhaps the worst, but by no means the only, grievance of the Indians around the Whitman mission. An especially harsh winter in 1846–7 had already reduced their numbers and heightened their anxiety. They didn't understand why American women were reluctant to marry Indians, although white men routinely took Indian brides and consorts. Finally, a Dartmouth-educated native named Tom Hill had been warning his people for some time that settlers migrating to the Walla Walla Valley would steal their lands.

Despite repeated warnings of imminent attacks, Whitman failed to abandon his mission and flee to nearby Fort Walla Walla. On November 29, 1847, a Cayuse party led by Chief Tilaukaikt entered the mission and requested to speak with Whitman. When he welcomed them into the kitchen, he was tomahawked to death from behind. The attack spread throughout the complex, with buildings burned, Whitman's wife and twelve others murdered, and forty-seven men, women, and children taken prisoner. They were rescued by the respected Hudson's Bay manager Peter Skene Ogden—"Uncle Pete" to the natives—who negotiated the release of the hostages, seven oxen, and sixteen bags of flour in exchange for sixty-three cotton shirts, sixty-two blankets, twelve guns, 600 loads of ammunition, thirty-seven pounds of tobacco, and twelve flints.

Despite this negotiated settlement, the "Whitman Massacre," as it came to be known, set off the Cayuse War. Expecting more conflict, the Oregon territorial legislature formed a military company of 550 men. In February 1848, a militia under Colonel Cornelius Gilliam killed twenty neutral natives,

creating a wider conflict. A party of 250 Palouse retaliated one month later, wounding ten. Gilliam and his men eventually returned to their homes as the conflict sputtered along.

In 1850, with U.S troops and more settlers arriving, five Cayuse—one of whom was not involved in the Whitman attack or murders—surrendered. Asked why they had given themselves up, the massacre leader Tilaukaikt said, "Do not your missionaries teach us that Christ died to save his people? Thus we die, if we must, to save our people." They were hanged on June 3, bringing an end to the Cayuse War.

Nonetheless, the Cayuse, weakened by disease and attacks, continued to die off. Authorities forfeited Cayuse land to settlers. Some surviving Cayuse joined their neighboring Umatilla at a reservation on Oregon's Umatilla River or merged with

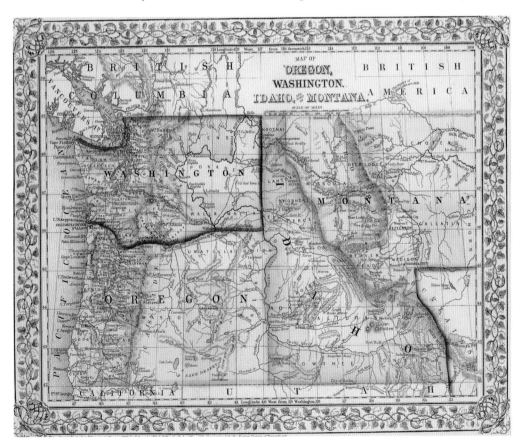

Left: This late-nineteenth-century map shows state borders and place names that reflect the distribution of major Native American tribes at this time.

Right: *Men working the Umatilla reclamation project to create the Cold Springs, Oregon, reservoir in 1907. Such projects aided the settlers, but impinged on the lands and resources of the Native Americans of the region.*

the Nez Percé and Yakima tribes. One of the war's tragedies was the needless suffering of non-Cayuse Indians, who were soon headed en masse for reservations, their cultures broken, their numbers depleted, their lands lost. The Nez Percé in particular distanced themselves from the massacre and sought peace.

Even while the five Cayuse were being hanged, trouble was brewing elsewhere in the Northwest. Indians harassed travelers on the California Trail so fiercely that in 1850 Oregon's territorial governor Joseph Lane met with them on the Rogue River, in southwestern Oregon. He was accompanied by thirty men, including fifteen Klikitat. Two chiefs and seventy-five warriors arrived, by agreement, unarmed, as was the Lane party. A circle was formed, with the negotiators in the middle. Before talks could begin, however, another party of Rogue River Indians, armed with bows and guns, joined the parley. Sensing trouble, Lane and some of the other Klikitat moved closer to the primary chief. When the chief bellowed his objections to Lane's proposals, and 150 braves stood

up, issuing war cries, Lane had his braves pin the chief down, with a knife held at his throat. The unflappable governor walked a gauntlet of hostile natives, tipping their leveled guns with his revolver. On Lane's orders, the captive chief told his troops to lay down their arms and withdraw. Kept as a hostage, he later agreed to Lane's terms and called himself Chief Jo in Lane's honor.

But peace could last only so long. In 1853 the first Rogue River War broke out in southwestern Oregon. Again, conflict was touched off by a tragic misunderstanding. In August, settlers, wrongly suspecting Rogue River natives of thievery, attacked their camp. Naturally, the Indians responded by attacking settlers. American volunteers and soldiers drove the natives into the Cascade Mountains. After a massive battle on August 24, the Treaty of Table Rock was signed, again with considerable drama. This time Lane and ten unarmed companions faced off with 700 fully armed natives. When a naked brave arrived with news that a subchief had been shot, many Indians considered reacting in kind.

Seated on a log, Lane issued a soothing speech condemning any reprisals and promising justice for the killers and compensation for the tribe. Their tempers cooled, the Rogue River Indians yielded all their land and agreed to live on a reservation.

In 1855, when many natives wandered from the reservations and leaders like Old John agitated for revenge, the second Rogue River War began. In one case, volunteers fired by night on an Indian camp in the Cascades. The next day they discovered that they had killed twenty-three old men, women and children. Using secret trails and often fighting with superior rifles, the natives attacked and virtually obliterated settlements, driving settlers into forts. By the winter of 1855–6, government troops were scouring the hills for warriors and burning camps. "It has become a contest of extermination by both whites and Indians," said General John E. Wool, U.S. commander in the Pacific Northwest.

The following spring, Colonel Robert C. Buchanan formed three columns for a final offensive. Meeting with him on May 21, some chiefs promised to quit fighting, but Old John stood firm. The decisive battle—which could have gone either way—was fought on May 27–8 at Big Meadows in southwestern Oregon. Holding off Old John's 200 warriors, 85 soldiers under Andrew J. Smith, lacking food, water, or shelter, were isolated on a hill by nightfall. They were rescued the following day by reinforcements sent by Buchanan. Following the American victory at Big Meadows, Buchanan's troops swept down the Rogue River toward Port Oxford, capturing some 400 Indian prisoners en route. The troops shot or drowned those too weak to march.

Eventually, 1,200 Indians were confined to the Coast Reservation. Deserted and defeated, the much-feared Old John finally surrendered on June 29, ending the nine-month war. He was imprisoned far away, in California's Fort Alcatraz.

Meanwhile, there was warfare north of the Columbia River. Washington had become a separate territory in 1853, and two years later its governor, Isaac Ingalls Stevens, decided to remove all Indians to reservations. A treaty to that end had been signed, but even the friendly Nez Percé felt they had been tricked. Discovery of gold on the Columbia River, bringing hordes of miners into

Below: A Cayuse woman and her horse. Marcus Whitman established a Presbyterian mission among the Cayuse in Washington, but was killed in an uprising.

Washington Territory, crowded the natives even more. When rumors spread that a Yakima chief named Kamiakin was preparing for war, Major Granville O. Haller headed for the Yakima Valley with 150 soldiers. The Yakima War was about to begin.

Kamiakin was indeed hoping to preserve control of the territory's central plateau, and in October 1855, the sides clashed about fifty miles north of the Columbia. Crushed by a superior force of 500 natives, the American soldiers fell back to The Dalles with the loss of five

men, a howitzer, and most of their supplies, provisions, and horses. Oregon militia got into the fray by murdering a Walla Walla chief at a peace meeting. At this point, there was no unanimity among settlers. Asahel Bush, writing for the *Oregon Statesman,* derided reports

of fighting, claiming that they were excuses to raid the federal treasury. Wool, the commander of the Pacific region, accused Governor Stevens of fomenting war as an excuse to seize Indian lands.

Kamiakin avoided further encounters until winter set in, but the his tribe remained so threatening that Fort Walla Walla was abandoned, with some of its munitions thrown into a river. The remainder of the ammunition was entrusted to a friendly Walla Walla chief, and local ranchers were told to head for settlements. On December 7, 1856, a date that shall certainly live in infamy among Washington Native Americans, a four-day battle began near Waiilatpu. The Indians were scattered, and Chief Peupeumoxmox scalped, with his ears pickled. The soldiers barely got through the winter, freezing and living on stores dug from Indian caches, before reinforcements arrived in March.

When Kamiakin and his allies withdrew, a shaky peace lasted through 1857. In 1858, however, more gold was discovered in eastern Washington, bringing with it prospectors, settlers, and tensions. Two forces faced each other. From the west came 164 infantry and cavalrymen led by Lieutenant Colonel Edward J. Steptoe to protect the miners; from the east were greater numbers of Yakima, Palouse, Spokane, and Coeur d'Alene warriors. Steptoe retreated, but on May 17, the Indians attacked. Outnumbered and beaten, his troops down to three rounds of ammunition, Steptoe was allowed to bury his dead and depart. Soon afterward, another column of regulars under Colonel George Wright set out to avenge Steptoe's humiliation.

On September 1, the Battle of Four Lakes, ten miles south of Spokane, was a

Left: *Oregon's Rogue River. Indians of this name fought two brutal wars inspired at least in part by settlers encroaching on their lands.*

Right: *A Klamath man praying to the spirits of Oregon's Crater Lake. Also known as Deep Blue Lake for its color, Crater embodied the intense spirituality of the Klamath, who used shamans to care for the sick.*

crushing blow for the natives. Wright's regulars inflicted long-range rifle damage, followed by a cavalry charge. U.S. forces lost no one and reported sixty Indian deaths. Four days later, at the Battle of Spokane Plain, Wright finished off the allied resistance. To ensure this victory, he seized Indian leaders, summarily executed fifteen of them, and sent the wounded Kamiakin fleeing to the mountains. The Cayuse and Yakima Wars destroyed any further resistance to American control of Washington and Oregon. Even Kamiakin spent his last years on a reservation.

The penultimate Indian war in the Northwest was fought over California's Lost River Valley. Surrounding Lake Tule at the California-Oregon border, it was inhabited by perhaps 1,000 Modoc. Beginning in the 1850s, however, white settlers began flooding in to build ranches on the rich grasslands. The Modoc resisted, first in armed conflict, then by stealing horses and cattle. In 1864 they were forced onto a Klamath reservation that was located some 25 miles north of the Oregon border.

Trouble flared up immediately. The Modoc and Klamath were long-standing enemies, and the Modoc hated reservation life. In the late 1860s, their leader Kintpuash, called Captain Jack by settlers, returned to his homeland with about 500 followers. They were forced back to the reservation, but in 1870 Kintpuash and 225 followers returned to their home in northern California.

Within two years, pressure from the settlers induced the Indian Bureau to send in the U.S. cavalry. The war was bound to end as it did, because 1,000 cavalrymen confronted some 75 warriors and 150 women and children. Nevertheless, the Modoc scored some notable victories. They were better organized than the U.S. forces, which had been summoned from Oregon's Fort Klamath virtually unprepared. On January 17, 1873, Lieutenant Colonel Frank Wheaton's forces attacked a trapped Modoc contingent in the lava fields below Tule Lake. The area was called the Land of Burnt-out Fires, and the soldiers had to ride through fog to face a hidden foe. By sunset, the Modoc had killed nine and wounded twenty-eight in the Battle of the Stronghold.

On April 11, Brigadier General Edward R.S. Canby ignored warnings of treachery to meet with Kintpuash and his representatives. The Indian leader asked the general to remove his soldiers and leave the Modoc in California. Canby refused. Kintpuash then shot Canby in the face and stabbed him to death—the only U.S. general ever to perish in an

Overleaf: A Nez Percé war site. The tribe was pursued 1,500 miles from their homelands by U.S. troops. In the words of a Nez Percé woman, "we were fools and the white man's lies made us more foolish."

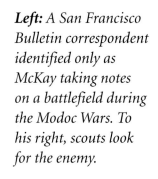

Left: A San Francisco Bulletin correspondent identified only as McKay taking notes on a battlefield during the Modoc Wars. To his right, scouts look for the enemy.

Right: General William Tecumseh Sherman. Known for his ruthlessness during the Civil War, he later became commanding general of the U.S. Army and vowed to obliterate the Modoc.

Indian war. And on April 26, twenty-two Modoc warriors, creeping out of crevices and caves in the lava fields, ambushed seventy-eight troops and killed twenty-five.

But winning skirmishes was not winning the war. By mid-May the Modoc, short of food and water, were reduced to squabbling, flight, or surrender. Surrounded by enemies, they gave up at last. On June 1, Kintpuash, his family and his last three loyal warriors were captured. By order of General William Tecumseh Sherman, who had plenty of experience razing property and scattering communities during the Civil War, the Modoc were effectively eradicated. Kintpuash and three other leaders were hanged on October 3, and 155 survivors were deported East on Sherman's explicit instructions, "so that the name Modoc shall cease." As harsh as this punishment was, it was more common practice throughout California to kill rather than relocate the Native Americans, with the result that there would be few left by the early twentieth century.

Right: Chief Joseph. The most famous of Nez Percé leaders, he surrendered in 1877 with the eloquent message, "I will fight no more forever."

The Northwest's last and perhaps most tragic conflict was the Nez Percé War of 1877. A tribe with a history of good relations with newcomers, the Nez Percé fought bravely against overwhelming odds, retreated 1,500 miles, and surrendered nobly and eloquently.

After helping Lewis and Clark, supplying horses and food to weary travelers on the Oregon Trail, and even furnishing cavalry to U.S. armies fighting other tribes, the Nez Percé were betrayed by U.S. government officials who turned their hunting and grazing grounds over to settlers and miners. An 1863 treaty broke the tribe into two groups, one content to accept payments and live on a reservation, the other, under Tuekakas—called Old Chief Joseph by settlers—composed of resistant stockmen and hunters.

The insurgents were first allowed to remain on the Wallowa River in eastern Oregon and Idaho, but in the mid-1870s the chief's successor and son, Hin-mah-too-yah-lat-keyt (Thunder Rolling Down from the Mountains), who was also called

INDIAN WARS

Chief Joseph, was forced onto Idaho's Lapwai Reservation. While he and his followers headed there in June 1877, disaffected warriors raided a settlement and killed four residents known to have mistreated Indians. When other warriors joined their force, which killed fifteen more settlers, the Nez Percé War was on.

A four-month struggle with an inevitable conclusion—there were 2,000 troops against 300 warriors protecting 500 old men, women, and children—the war was fiercely contested nonetheless. Some 180 Americans were killed and 150 wounded. Among the Nez Percé, at least 120 lost their lives. In the end, numerical superiority forced the tribes to flee 1,500 miles, narrowly averting capture more than once, through Idaho to Wyoming, Montana, and north. Ninety-eight warriors and about 200 women and children under Chief White Bird escaped north to Canada. Surrounded and outnumbered, lacking

ponies and food, Chief Joseph and the remaining 400 yielded to Colonel Nelson A. Miles, 40 miles south of the border on October 15, 1877.

Generals Miles and Oliver Howard promised the Indians a settlement on the Lapwai Reservation, but General Sherman later overruled them and dispersed the Nez Percé to reservations in three states. As he surrendered, Chief Joseph dictated a statement to a translator that included the moving elegy: "I am tired of fighting. Our chiefs are killed....The little children are freezing to death. My people, some of them, have run away to the hills, and have no blankets, no food....Hear me, my chiefs. I am tired. My heart is sick and sad. From where the sun now stands, I will fight no more forever."

As expressed by a Native American of the Northwest, these eloquent words, unfortunately, speak for nineteenth century Native Americans across the land.

Overleaf: Nez Percé homelands in Oregon and Idaho. The majority of survivors were initially dispersed among reservations in several states, where more died than those lost in all the battles.

Left: Nez Percé warriors. Even when outnumbered, they inflicted heavy casualties on their adversaries.

THE
NORTHWEST
AT WORK

Previous page:
A tailing wheel used in mining. This wheel, at the Kennedy Mine in Jackson, California, removed the "tailings," or waste, left after the ore was processed. The 1849 gold rush helped open up the West for settlement.

Below: A California miner in the 1849 gold rush. Few of them made fortunes: many were washed out like so much fool's gold— minerals like pyrite mistaken for gold.

In the course of the nineteenth century, the Northwest developed into a region notable for spectacular natural resources and booming businesses. In Oregon, Washington, and northern California, there are no dust storms like those that tormented Oklahoma, nor boll weevils like those that once destroyed crops throughout the South. Indeed, the Northwest has flourished in agriculture, with fertile vegetable farms and fruit-bearing orchards spread about like colorful patches on a quilt. And conditions combined to make the region hospitable to many other occupations, including livestock ranching, fishing, lumbering, papermaking, shipping from ports accessible to the Far East, and railroading on lines connecting to the East Coast.

Of course, the Northwest didn't begin as a gigantic job fair. Its early explorers and settlers trafficked in the most rudimentary forms of hunting, fishing, trapping, farming, animal husbandry, and mining. Sea otters were the original attraction for Europeans seeking fur-bearing animals along the Northwest coast, but if there was a symbol of the working Northwest, it was the beaver. More than anything else, the furry creature with the flat tail attracted the first rough-and-ready characters and their trapping companies to the area. How intrinsic was the beaver to the culture of the Northwest? Consider this: after gold ore was discovered in California, Oregonians were spared the inconvenience of weighing gold dust by a currency called "beaver money." Five- and ten-dollar gold pieces manufactured by the Oregon Exchange Company, they were technically illegal (because not authorized by the government), but undeniably useful. And everyone recognized the creature embossed on them.

Europeans, including the Russians, and early Americans along the Northwest coast, exhausted the sea otter population by about 1800, and beaver became virtually the only game in town for regional trappers. Beaver colonies had coexisted with Native Americans, who used them for food and fur without depleting their numbers. When Americans and British began contesting the area late in the eighteenth century, however, it was an open question whether they favored the land or beaver pelts. After Lewis and Clark traveled through the Northwest in 1804–6, trappers and hunters—many of them from Canada—dominated the region for almost fifty years.

First, they captured beaver any way they could: by shooting them, snaring them, ripping apart their dams and clubbing them. The popular steel trap invented by Sewall Newhouse in 1823

was used extensively. At one point, competition raged so fiercely that John McLoughlin, the chief agent for Great Britain's Hudson's Bay Company, urged his trappers to deplete the population before the Yanks could get to it. They annihilated not only the beavers, but the marvelous wetlands created by them.

As the Native Americans had, newcomers relished beavers for their food too. "Among prime frontier delicacies not to be had any more are beavers," Nancy Wilson Ross wrote in her midtwentieth century book *Farthest Reach: Oregon & Washington*. "Trappers were very partial to the meat of a fat beaver, particularly beaver leg, roasted and sliced off cold, which was considered equal to the finest pig. Then there were beaver tails cut up in chunks, with the bones removed, the 'meat all tender and jelly-like' eaten with hunks of smoky bread." She goes on to report that Lewis and Clark's journal contained an "astonishing" description of how to catch a beaver. It involved a delicate surgical operation on one beaver in order to remove the "bark-stone" that yielded the castor, an oily, odorous substance. Trappers also carried a supply of cloves, nutmeg, and cinnamon: the scent of both spices and castor attracted beavers from miles away. But it was beaver fur that turned a far greater profit—that is, until around 1850, when beaver went out of style in hatmaking and silk began to replace it. The beaver survived, and Northwesterners looked to other occupations.

Another natural resource of the region, gold, figured prominently in its development. Despite the evanescent nature of gold and silver mining—the boom-or-bust cycle of mines and mining towns built and abandoned, jobs

created and lost, some fortunes made amid general failure—the mining business should not be underrated. For one thing, not all that glitters need be gold. In Washington's Cascade Mountains, for example, copper and coal as well as gold were dug out of the ground (and still are). In addition, the fifty-year "rush"—from California in 1848–9 to Alaska in 1897–8—generated substantial revenue, many ancillary occupations, and much immigration. The mania for minerals filled up a great expanse that had previously been left to Native Americans, Mexicans, and a very small number of traders and trappers. The "gold rush" was really the rush to the West.

Several hundred thousand Americans, Europeans, Latin Americans, and Chinese flooded northern California after gold was discovered at Sutter's Mill near Sacramento in January 1848. Early results were so encouraging that two-thirds of the men then working in Oregon, plus thousands more from Hawaii, Mexico, Peru, and Chile, arrived in California before the year's end. The influx swelled in 1849 with the arrival of thousands

Above: Miners crossing the Chilkoot Pass in Alaska during the second most-famous gold rush (1897–8) in American history. As a base for gold seekers heading north, Seattle grew in population from 40,000 to 200,000 in about twelve years and established itself on a par with Portland.

Overleaf: The Kennedy Mine County Historical Park near Sierra City, California.

Far left: Malikoff-Diggings Historic Park, near North Bloomfield, California, reveals the erosion patterns in the rock formed by hydraulic mining.

Left: A Wells Fargo Express building in Columbia, California.

Below: Old mining equipment displayed in Downieville, California.

from the eastern part of the United States and still others from the British Empire.

At first miners simply "panned" for gold. After dislodging dirt and gravel with a pick and shovel, they put the debris in a circular pan, added water, and swirled the pan. The water rinsed off the dirt and gravel, leaving heavier gold at the bottom. Soon rockers or "cradles" washed more efficiently than pans. Later, adding mercury to amalgamate with gold saved precious minerals from washing away. Finally, long wooden troughs known as sluices caught the gold flowing downstream through a series of boxes. At first, individuals recorded land claims that were available for purchase. By the end of the 1850s, mining companies had taken over these businesses, bringing with them demands for capital outlay, complex machinery, and skilled labor that ended the careers of unskilled prospectors.

To be sure, it did help to arrive in California as quickly as possible. "My girls can make from 5 to 25 dollars per day washing gold in pans," an early miner wrote relatives in Missouri. "My

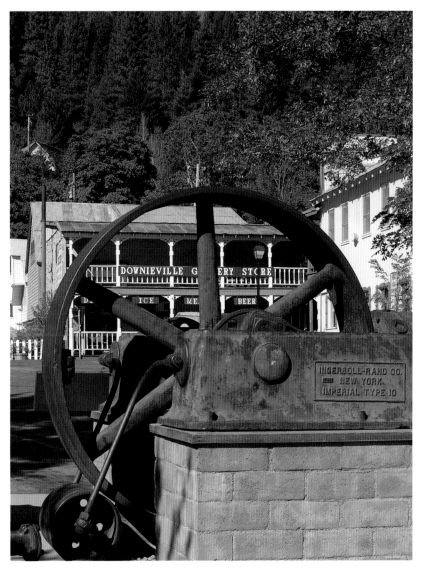

101

average income this winter will be about 150 dollars a day." Not everyone fared so well. The average wage of a miner may have been about $20 in 1848 and $16 in 1849, but it dwindled to $3 by the late 1850s. Though about $200 million-worth of gold was dug up, there were certainly more cases of individual failure than success. But many non-miners profited in other ways, too. According to *The New Encyclopedia of the American West*, "Wherever they went, the gold rush crowds attracted merchants in great numbers; freighting, stagecoach and express companies; skilled craftsmen, especially of the metal trades; lawyers; newspaper publishers; politicians eager to create offices that they themselves might fill; and the saloonkeepers, gamblers, 'madams,' and 'bad men' that dominate fictional portrayals." Although many of these people found their services unwanted after the boom passed, they stayed on—after both the California and Alaska gold rushes—and some, at least, became important contributors to the development of the Northwestern region.

Wagon and stagecoach lines, shipping, and railroads also serviced the gold-rush population. Some Western cities, like San Francisco and Denver, grew up around the gold rush. Others, like Salt Lake City, Portland, and Seattle ably accommodated miners headed elsewhere. The example of Seattle is especially noteworthy. A July 17, 1894, telegram announced that "The Steamship *Portland* has just arrived in Seattle [from Alaska] with a ton of gold on board." Suddenly, failed miners from California, Oregon, and Colorado were looking for adventure up north. The *Portland* returned to Alaska filled with passengers. Clearly, Seattle could benefit from becoming the jumping-off point for prospectors, or "sourdoughs," as they were called for the coarsely textured bread they made. Everything from stores to houses of prostitution sprang up to service and supply the travelers. When

Right: A reef netter boat and the Shaw Island Historical Society building in Washington's San Juan Islands. Fishing by net became a Puget Sound industry during the nineteenth century.

Seattle named Asa Brainerd as its publicist, the former newspaper editor printed advertisements in publications the world over. By the time Alaskan gold lost its luster early in the twentieth century, the sleepy little town on Elliott Bay had grown to rival long-established Portland.

Agriculture was a natural career change for the retired miners. Many became cattle ranchers. From the Willamette Valley in western Oregon, settlers moved to the drier climate of northeastern Oregon, where livestock sold for twice as much. Eventually, sheep-raising outstripped cattle-raising. Flour was exported from the Columbia River to San Francisco, and from there to Japan, as early as 1857. Wheat crops flourished throughout the Oregon and Washington interior.

At first, agriculture was primitive: digging out tree stumps, plowing furrows behind oxen, and planting seeds. Great ranges and wandering herds were wasteful of both the land and the animals: hard winters and insufficient food wiped out cattle and sheep alike. Fortunately, irrigation came to the rescue. The region was ideal for it, thanks to the Columbia River and its tributaries, snowmelt from the mountains, lakes, streams, and natural locales for reservoirs. Early in the nineteenth century, the Hudson's Bay Company had irrigated its gardens, and Protestant and Catholic missionaries taught irrigation techniques to Native Americans. The Carey Act of 1894 helped Oregon to acquire and irrigate 432,203 acres of federal desert.

As a result, farming and orchards took over arid grazing land. Newly enriched, the soil sprouted agricultural products abundantly. The seed was planted for a famous apple tree in Vancouver,

Washington, back in 1825. William Meek brought the region's first grafted fruit trees to Hayward, California, in 1847, and farmers in Hood River, Oregon, planted fruit trees in 1854. Eventually orchards producing apples, cherries, peaches, and pears filled entire regions, including Oregon's Hood River Valley and Washington's Columbia Basin. By 1910 the national center of apple production had shifted from New York and Missouri to Oregon and Washington.

The Northwest's most notable fruit is probably the grape used for winemaking. California's vineyards became famous the world over. Although the great flowering of the wine industry did not occur until well into the twentieth century, some of the California vineyards got started in the late 1800s. Not to be overlooked were such places as the Christian Brothers Winery in St. Helena, Washington, and the Pickering Passage in Puget Sound, where wine grapes have been grown since 1879.

Above: The hardships of life on the frontier: a period photograph from Oregon shows a woman making soap from animal fat and wood ash.

Overleaf: Orchards in the Wenatchee River Valley near Cashmere, Washington. In the early twentieth century, Germany's kaiser refused to eat any but imported Wenatchee apples.

Above: Ripley's "Believe It Or Not" Museum is housed in a Santa Rosa, California, Baptist church said to have been built of lumber from a single redwood tree in 1874.

attracted people to the area, the industry took off. In 1884 the mills around Washington's Puget Sound processed one million boards of Douglas fir every day. By 1890 one billion board feet were being felled and milled. With other trees like Western hemlock, Western red cedar, and Sitka spruce contributing to the logging industry, Washington became the nation's leading lumber state in 1905. And lumber was another industry that created additional business. In 1874 the introduction of many large sailing ships made deep-water Puget Sound towns excellent ports for trading with Asia, which is several hundred miles closer to Washington than to California. Seattle and Tacoma suddenly found themselves thriving ports for lumber and logs shipped off to locations as distant as Chile, China, Australia, and Argentina. Not to mention California, which unloaded 200 million board feet in 1883 and 1884 and 323 million in 1889. But the Northwest's prime port was Seattle, which was located on the shortest line for silk trade between New York and Yokohama.

Amid such growth and development came early calls for conservation. In 1864 Congress gave the Yosemite Valley to California "for public use, resort and recreation," creating one of the nation's first national parks. Interestingly, the land was made available because it was deemed to have little economic usefulness. Sequoia National Park (1890), Muir Woods (1908), and the Point Reyes National Seashore give northern California a well-deserved reputation for being at the forefront of conservation. Moreover, in the country's most populous state, it is notable that vast reaches of northern California are still under-

Fishing became a major industry in the Northwest. The area was best known for salmon, which the Native Americans had been taking from the Columbia and other rivers for thousands of years. The canned variety of this salmon became one of the most popular staples in the world, but halibut, cod, and herring were not far behind. Shellfish and crustaceans from the Northwest coast also became highly prized catches.

Another symbol of the Northwest was the Bunyanesque, strapping lumberman. Logging came naturally to the Northwest, which was filled with giant coniferous trees. Once the gold rush

populated. (Modoc County, in north-east California, is the size of Connecticut yet still has fewer than 9,000 people.) Washington has seven national parks and forests, and Oregon has almost two dozen federally protected forests, parks, monuments, and wildlife sanctuaries.

Another symbol of the Northwest is the great Western railroad network. Indeed, the railway connection between East and West can be said to be rooted here: it was a number of northern Californians—Leland Stanford, Charles Crocker, Mark Hopkins, and Collis P. Huntington—who helped take the lead in planning and financing the first great transcontinental railroad. On May 10, 1869, Irish-born immigrants working westward for the Union Pacific met Chinese immigrants working east for the Central Pacific at Promontory Point,

Above: *The "Oregon Pony," built in 1861 by the Vulcan Iron Works, was used by the Oregon Portage Railway. It has been on display at Oregon's Cascade Locks since 1970.*

Left: *Chinese workers building the Central Pacific Railroad. On May 10, 1869, Chinese laborers working east met Irish crews working west at Promontory Point, Utah, to connect the country's first transcontinental railroad.*

Right: Late-summer corn tassels in Snohomish Valley, Washington.

Opposite: A Yosemite Valley, California, oak tree in the spring. One of America's first national parks, Yosemite was also the site of a valley used as a dam and reservoir for San Francisco.

Below: The Mill Creek Vineyards near Healdsburg, California. The Golden State's wineries, begun in the late 1800s, have become equal to those of Europe.

Above: *A period photograph of an exploited young Chinese immigrant in California—displaced, alone, and vulnerable.*

Utah. Four symbolic spikes—two gold, one silver, another made of gold, silver and iron—were tapped into position. Then a simple iron spike, wired to a telegraph key, was to be pounded home by Leland Stanford of the Central Pacific line. He swung—and missed. Nonetheless, the telegrapher signaled "Done!" A great cheer rose from a telegraph office in Washington, D.C., and an illuminated ball descended from the Capitol dome. In Philadelphia, the Liberty Bell rang. And in San Francisco, a new banner announced: "California annexes the United States."

What a moment! No more would all travelers have to sail around South America, or take Conestoga wagons (named for the Pennsylvania town where they were made) across arid plains and rugged mountains. Nor would mail be carried exclusively by still another Western symbol immortalized in so many motion pictures—the Pony Express. This service began on April 3, 1860, from St. Joseph, Missouri, to Sacramento, California, advertising delivery by relay riders for $5 an ounce in no more than ten days. In fact, a ten-

day journey would have cut in half the time that the Overland Mail Company route had established by stagecoach, and 190 way stations were set up 10 to 15 miles apart to service horse and rider. The mail was wrapped in protective oiled silk and fit into a leather flap on the saddle. Western movies notwithstanding, the Pony Express took seventeen or eighteen days, failed financially, and lasted only eighteen months.

For its part, the stagecoach had a longer life. Operating in the United States from 1785, when a line began carrying passengers between New York City and Albany, New York, the cumbersome British-made coaches and rutted roads got along about as well as a Redcoat and a Minuteman. An improved American vehicle, with better suspension and a lower center of gravity, was unveiled by Lewis Downing and J. Stephen Abbot in 1826. Weighing 2,500 pounds, retailing for $1,500, the Concord coach (for the town in New Hampshire where it was first made) was outfitted for nine passengers with such amenities as scrollwork and gold-leafed interiors. Conducting his six horses like a maestro, the reinsman (also known as the whip or jehu), held the reins of the two lead horses between his fore- and middle fingers, the middle horses between his middle and third fingers, and the two rear "wheelers" between his third and little fingers. The first Western stagecoach line, Oregon's "Telegraph Line," was opened by S.H.L. Meek in 1846 and profited when the gold rush sent people "Westward ho!" Before the transcontinental railroad was completed in 1869, many stagecoach companies—the most famous being Wells, Fargo—competed strenuously, and isolated gold strikes kept them going for decades.

Another distinctive mode of transportation associated with the Northwest are San Francisco's cable cars, introduced in 1871. They made—and continue to make—treks up hills more enjoyable and have become a civic emblem. But conventional railroads figured most prominently in the development of the Northwest. Thanks to one railroad man, Henry Villard, Portland preceded Seattle as the first great city of the Northwest. As mentioned earlier, Villard placed Northwestern exhibits at the Philadelphia Centennial celebration of 1876, championing Oregon (he had an immigration bureau in Portland) and siphoning away homesteaders who might otherwise have headed to California. The following year, 18,000 newcomers came to Oregon. In 1884, when Villard established Portland as the western terminus of the Northern Pacific railroad, the city's future was assured. His trains shipped lumber to Montana, Colorado, and Iowa, and Portland quickly grew into what historian Dorothy Johansen has called "the web of commerce and culture" of the upper Northwestern region.

Villard had promised to extend his line to Tacoma and Seattle, but he went broke. Not until 1884 did the Northern Pacific, under new management, extend to Tacoma. And not until 1892 did Seattle get a line of its own—James J. Hill's Great Northern. Even then, freight rates were more favorable to Oregon. It was not until the Alaskan gold strike that Seattle established itself on a par with Portland.

Who were the Northwesterners who did all this work and created the sturdy and vibrant region that entered the twentieth century? There was some variety, including Basque sheepherders and farmers in Eastern Oregon and Jews recruited to Oregon farming communes by the Hebrew Emigrant Aid Society. But the Northwest was generally homogeneous—and for all the wrong reasons. Native Americans, herded onto reservations, were virtually invisible to the newly dominant society. Oregon passed, then rescinded, the fourteenth Amendment granting citizenship to African Americans—and did not approve the Fifteenth Amendment guaranteeing them suffrage until 1959. Immigration to Oregon from the East and

Below: A nineteenth-century Chinese laundry in California. Because of restrictive laws, Chinese immigrants to American cities were herded into "Chinatowns."

Midwest did nothing to change attitudes. The white citizens of the ironically named Liberty, Oregon, banished all African Americans in 1893. Not until they arrived on the railroads as porters and waiters did they make a dent in Oregon's population, mainly in Portland.

Oregon and Washington clamored for the expulsion of the Chinese. In 1885 Tacoma residents rounded up Chinese immigrants and shipped them to Portland. A year later Washington forbade them to own property. In Seattle, 350 Chinese were "escorted" to the waterfront for shipment down to San Francisco. A writ of habeas corpus halted the proceedings, but most of the Chinese, seeing persecution and violence ahead, boarded the ship and sailed for California—where they were also mistreated. Despite the vibrant Chinese community, the most active in the New World, all-white unions were formed in the 1860s and '70s in opposition to Chinese and Hispanic workers. Further, the Chinese Exclusion Act of 1882 reduced immigration and forced Chinese into small areas known as Chinatowns. Soon enough, enclaves would be formed to isolate Japanese, Irish, and Italian newcomers as well.

Racism was an unfortunate aspect of the region's burgeoning prosperity. By 1900 the Northwest was producing wealth from its mountains, rivers, plains, rolling farmland, and irrigated desert, but many of its people were less welcoming than the land. However, the twentieth century would offer a second chance for the Northwest to diversify its population.

Below: Oregon's fruitful Hood River Valley, with Mount Hood looming over orchards in their finest autumn colors.

THE
TWENTIETH
CENTURY

The twentieth century in the Northwest opened with everything from gala celebrations to unmitigated disasters. At 5:13 AM on April 18, 1906, a gigantic earthquake in San Francisco rippled into history. Wrenching off the Pacific floor, racing at two miles per second, it rocked a schooner 150 miles out to sea; sent seismographs jumping as far away as South Africa, England, Russia, and Japan; and all but pulverized the city by the bay.

"There was a deep rumbling, deep and terrible, and then I could see it actually coming up Washington Street," Jesse Cook, a local police sergeant, was quoted in *The San Francisco Earthquake,* by Gordon Thomas and Max Morgan Witts. "The whole street was undulating. It was as if the waves of the ocean were rumbling towards me, billowing as they came."

A few blocks away, John Barrett, an editor at the *Examiner,* heard a moan that had buildings "dancing." Said Barrett: "It was as though the earth was slipping quietly away under our feet. There was a sickening sway, and then we were flat on our faces." Even prone, he could tell that the *Examiner* and other buildings were swaying onto the street, then rocking back repeatedly. "Trolley tracks were twisted, their wires down, wriggling like serpents, flashing blue sparks all the time," Barrett added. "The street was gashed in any number of places. From some of the holes water was spurting; from others, gas."

Two- to three-foot waves of earth plowed through the streets, knocking down everything that lay in their path. Aftershocks were strong enough to obliterate whole forests of giant redwoods. A full four days of fire followed the quake, and the total damage it wreaked was staggering: 28,000 buildings were destroyed, 700 people killed and another quarter-million homeless. (Hundreds more died in areas up and down the 650-mile-long San Andreas Fault extending north and south of the city.)

The earthquake and the ensuing fire, easily the most famous event in San Francisco history, was both a disaster and a wake-up call. Once the citizenry sorted out their jumble of reactions—some residents stumbled outside, speechless, in their sleeping clothes; others retreated to Golden Gate Park; still others, both residents and outsiders, looted—San Franciscans mobilized. Over the next four years, they set about rebuilding the San Francisco that would become a modern center of finance, manufacturing, and international trade. So many new towns were built in its vicinity that San Francisco developed into a metropolitan area as well as a city. In 1915 the Panama-Pacific International Exposition showcased it as a gateway to the world.

That was not all. In a region noted for outstanding universities, no place could top the Bay Area, whose most famous institutions were the University of California, Berkeley, and Stanford University in Palo Alto. San Francisco itself would support several fine universities. The Bay Area was also a haven for such creative individuals as the writers Jack London and John Steinbeck.

Perhaps its best-known landmark would be the notorious prison on Alcatraz Island. Located in the Bay, but always connected in popular lore to the city, it had served as the base for the West Coast's oldest lighthouse before it became a U.S. Army post and prison from the 1850s to 1934. That year it was converted into a federal prison, which housed many celebrated criminals. Among the 1,545 who lived on "The Rock" were Al Capone, "Machine Gun" Kelly, and the "Birdman of Alcatraz," Robert Stroud (although he never practiced his avian studies there).

Alcatraz became a federal lockdown thanks to the collaboration of U.S. Attorney General Homer Cummings and Director of Prisons Sanford Bates. Cummings specifically sought "a special prison for kidnappers, racketeers, and individuals guilty of predatory crimes," according to the Alcatraz Web Page. Only two prisoners escaped successfully without being captured or found dead later, but it is doubtful they survived long in the treacherous waters. Alcatraz closed down on March 21, 1963, the victim of high costs and a changing federal philosophy that favored rehabilitation. Said the last prisoner to leave, Frank Wathernam, "Alcatraz was never no good for nobody."

Portland and Seattle also rose from the ashes—in one case literally, in the other, metaphorically. Rebounding from a financial panic in 1893 and a depression that lasted until 1896, Portland benefited from the 1897–8 Alaska gold rush (though not as much as Seattle) and built so many gardens it became known as the "City of Roses." The $25-million Lewis and Clark Exposition of 1905, commemorating the 100th anniversary

Above: Originally named La Isla de los Alcatraces ("Island of the Pelicans") in 1775, Alcatraz became known simply as "the Rock" when its legendary maximum-security prison housed some of the world's most notorious criminals.

Right: Washington's Grand Coulee Dam. Built between 1933-41, it is still North America's largest concrete structure.

Opposite: California's Napa Valley vineyards. Opened in the mid-nineteenth century, their vineyards' first grapes of choice were called zinfandels, a name of unknown origin. Zinfandel wine is still known as "California's grape."

of the year the explorers reached the Northwest, boasted 385 acres of walks, lakes, and buildings contributed by several states and nations.

Seattle, after suffering an 1889 fire that destroyed most of the city center, rebuilt itself, became the terminus of the Great Northern Railroad, and joined the Union—all in a matter of months. The 1893 depression set the city back, but it boomed anew as the point of departure for the 1897–8 gold rush to Alaska. A decade of growth followed, and in 1909 Seattle opened its A-Y-P (Alaska-Yukon-Pacific) Exposition, which drew nearly four million visitors over a four-month period. The next year Seattle's population exceeded Portland's by 30,000. Suddenly, the Pacific Northwest—or New Eden—was the place to be.

What all three cities—and the region—shared during the first decades of the twentieth century was an extraordinary modernization. To say they began the 1900s as frontier towns would be to exaggerate, but not by much. Without quibbling over the semantics, it is possible to examine some of the many ways in which the region changed dramatically.

Agriculture was no longer the gentle, pastoral occupation of yore. In 1902 Congress passed the fateful Newlands Reclamation Act, which authorized the Bureau of Reclamation to irrigate farmland and construct major dams like the Grand Coulee, Bonneville, and McNary. With the dams came equally modern fixtures like hydroelectricity, cement factories, flood control, reservoirs, and camp cities. At the time, dam builders and conservationists were allies. In their "stream-flow" philosophy, it was believed that forests would slow runoff from storms and melting snow, allowing water to be captured by dams and reservoirs, which, in turn, would supply irrigation. Future problems with irrigation—for example, reduced water levels threatening endangered species of fish—simply weren't appreciated at the time.

California, especially, benefited from reclamation projects, many of which depended on water brought down from the Northwest. By 1959 the state was a national leader in the value of agriculture-related products, producing 36 percent of the nation's vegetables, except potatoes; 26 percent of berries and small fruits, and 42 percent of U.S. orchard fruits and nuts. California was also a leader in poultry, cotton, and dairy products.

Agricultural machinery was also modernized quickly. The use of efficient reapers/threshers for harvesting and grain elevators for storage and shipping made the United States the "granary of the world." What had been primarily an east-of-the Rockies industry changed when extensions of the Northern Pacific and Great Northern Railroads pushed the wheat frontier out to the Pacific. Northwestern farmers created huge checkerboard fields filled with valuable crops ranging from peas, strawberries, beets, and potatoes to wine grapes and table flowers. Dairy farming changed especially. Replacing early-morning milking by hand were electrical milking machines, pipelines to trucks, gutter cleaners, manure spreaders, and silos for corn and hay storage, among other innovations. To own and operate machines like these, farmers needed to enlarge their herds and their land holdings. Stressed for credit, they turned to Congress for measures like the Federal Land Bank System (1916) and the Intermediate Credits Act (1923). During the Great Depression of the 1930s, the region also benefited greatly from the Emergency Mortgage Relief and Farm Credit Acts (both passed in 1933).

Lumbering, long a major industry in the area, moved into big-time produc-

tion during the first half of the twentieth century. To be sure, the work remained hard and dangerous—according to some estimates, the most dangerous industry in the nation. In the back country, workers had to watch out for shifting logs, loose chains that flew off the logs they were supposed to bind, and dead limbs, or "widow-makers." Once logs were delivered to mills and ports, production methods were more streamlined. Before freighters exported the lumber to ports as distant as Japan, jet streams of water ripped the bark from trees, and giant saws sliced them up. Coos Bay, Oregon, located on the largest harbor between Puget Sound and San Francisco, became what it bragged was "the world's largest lumber shipping port." Elsewhere, huge processing mills converted wood into plywood, paper, and other products. Not only was there more lumber being harvested, but more people were working in the woods. During the Depression, the Civilian Conservation Corps (1933–42) employed

Above: Nineteenth-century loggers in the Northwest cut down countless trees and wasted large amounts of wood without much thought, but during the twentieth century, loggers became much more conscious of the renewal of forest resources.

Opposite: Grand sequoias in the Calaveras (California) Big Trees State Park. The world's largest living things, sequoias are honored on the logo of the Sierra Club.

Right: *A former salmon cannery in Washington's San Juan Islands.*

Opposite: *Squalicum Harbor in Bellingham, Washington, with Mount Baker in the distance. Exemplifying Washington's reputation as a recreational center, the harbor has a marina filled with pleasure and charter boats, while Mount Baker accommodates a popular ski area and national forest.*

thousands of young men in planting trees, building roads and erosion dams, and fighting forest fires.

Construction now became a major industry. If there was no Empire State Building, there were plenty of other Bunyanesque feats. In Seattle, city engineer Roland H. Thompson took millions of tons of soil from the hills and dumped them in Elliott Bay as landfill to create waterfront structures and commercial sites. Although San Francisco's Golden Gate Bridge (1937) would become world-famous as the epic structure of the Northwest, "The City" was also developing lesser known but notable areas like Fisherman's Wharf, and constructing skyscrapers and luxury hotels.

The Northwest's coastline, such a scourge to early travelers, was finally conquered. Commercial fishing was, and is, a highly dangerous occupation, with such hazards as being washed overboard, snared in equipment, or capsized in storms—none of which prevented fishing vessels from adapting the latest technological innovations and expanding their hauls dramatically. The coast was dotted with lighthouses and safe harbors from which people ventured forth in yachts and other pleas-

ure boats. The same story was playing out inland. Astoria, Oregon, developed a notable canning industry for its bountiful salmon catch. Boats called purse seiners dragged vertically hung nets around Puget Sound, and Seattle constructed the Lake Washington Ship Canal. Recreational activities, from trout fishing to canoeing to water skiing, became even more prevalent in fresh water than on the ocean.

The three Northwestern regions had much in common, especially in the three major cities. Outstanding buildings and such urban centers as Pioneer Square in Seattle were constructed, and in line with the European model, parks and gardens kept nature alive in the midst of the cities: Volunteer Park in Seattle; the International Rose Test Gardens in Portland; and Golden Gate Park in San Francisco. The latter deserves special notice. At 1,000 acres, Golden Gate is the largest man-made park in the world. Among its many features are the famous Japanese Tea Gardens, the Asian Art Museum, and the M.H. de Young Memorial Museum. The Northwest also developed excellent smaller cities like the state capitals in Olympia, Washington; in Salem, Oregon; and in Sacramento,

Above: A view of
Second Avenue and
Yesler Way, in Seattle's
historic Pioneer Square
district, photographed
in 1904.

Opposite: El Capitan
in California's Yosemite
National Park. At
3,600 feet in elevation,
with a 3,000-foot
vertical face, El Cap
takes an average of four
days to scale.

California. Many cities provided attractive historic and cultural venues, among them the Lewis and Clark sculptures in Salem; in Spokane, Washington State's Riverfront Park; and Maryhill Castle in Maryhill, Washington.

But it would be misleading to suggest that the Northwest was a uniform area. According to political scientist Daniel J. Elazar, Oregon is one of nine "moralistic" states (the others are Maine, Vermont, Michigan, Wisconsin, Minnesota, North Dakota, Colorado, and Utah) whose leaders have evoked a passion for the public good. In addition to passing reforms that opened up the political process, Oregon's governor Oswald West (1911–15) once summoned the state militia to end gambling, drinking and vice in a wide-open boomtown east of the Cascades. In a more sensible act during his tenure, the Oregon legislature set aside the entire state coastline for "free and uninterrupted use" by the public in 1913.

Washington also began the twentieth century by endorsing several social reforms, ranging from direct primary elections to women's suffrage. However, reaction to labor unrest following World War I reduced interest in progressive legislation. Without a sound business base, unemployment set in, and with it considerable pressure to reduce the influx of immigrants. The Great Depression worsened matters and the federal government had to stabilize the state's economy with hydroelectric and irrigation dams.

California, meanwhile, would develop into the equivalent of two states—the conservative, populous, growth-oriented south and the liberal, more environmental north. While most early dams were built with little opposition, John Muir and his fellow environmentalists delayed construction of one across Yosemite National Park's Hetch Hetchy Valley for twelve years. Ultimately, the pressure for water to supply the San Francisco area won out, but conservationists lived to fight many other battles.

The Northwest's big cities embodied each region's distinctive culture. San Francisco became the center of West Coast sophistication and self-confidence. Testimony to this was the early construction of a symphony hall (1911) and an opera house (1923) by people who dressed in Parisian fashions and called their home "The City" as if there were no others. During World War II, the city's population surged when thousands of Americans relocated there to work in wartime industries. San Francisco eventually grew to 800,000 strong and finally embraced its considerable ethnic diversity. Internationalist in outlook from its beginnings, The City was the country's

number one port for Pacific-bound vessels during World War II and sponsored the formative United Nations Conference in 1945. San Franciscans loved their own hilly topography so much that they fought off extension of the Embarcadero Freeway inside the city limits. If there's a question about the city's endlessly good feelings, some might say its proud residents display a tendency to preen a bit over its many charms.

Seattle became a quintessentially growth-oriented American metropolis with its huge state university—the University of Washington—which was founded in 1861 and went on to become one of the major recipients of federal medical-research grants; high-rise buildings like the forty-two-story Smith Tower (1914); and big labor unions to combat big industrial management. In 1919 Seattle became the first city in the United States to have a general strike, when the Industrial Workers of the World (IWW) generated sympathy for the substandard conditions of loggers and shipyard workers. Seattle was subsequently rocked by the Depression, but recovered in part because of the multiengined planes built by the Boeing Airplane Company, established in 1916 when aviator William Boeing produced a pontoon biplane and later created the airline now known as United. By 1960 Boeing employed one of every ten residents within the Seattle metropolitan region; one in four Seattleites had a job affected by Boeing. (Later, dependence on largely undiversified industry would take a toll when Boeing cut back–eventually even moving its headquarters to Chicago!—but new enterprises, including Microsoft and Amazon.com, would become major new employers.)

Above: *San Francisco's Chinatown, a bustling neighborhood that is now a colorful tourist attraction.*

Opposite: *The 9,266-foot Golden Gate Bridge, with San Francisco in the background.*

Left: *The original Boeing factory in Seattle. A barometer of the city's economic status, it was long its major employer.*

125

Resembling a New England-style regional center rather than a major metropolis, Portland was named for Portland, Maine, when one of its two founders won a coin toss with his colleague from Boston, Massachusetts. The city prided itself on Reed College, an innovative institution founded with no intercollegiate sports, no attendance records, fraternities, sororities, or honor societies; a low-key, sometimes munificent business culture; and a lovely and accessible downtown. Charm positively flowed out of Portland. For the first six decades of the twentieth century, Italian vendors on Produce Row sold fresh meat, vegetables, fruits, and eggs from their farms in the old-world tradition.

Genteel looks can be deceiving, however. Following a brief interlude in which progressives produced direct-democracy reforms (initiatives, referendums, recalls), a corrupt business oligarchy smothered progress during the early twentieth century. For much of the 1920s, Portland was the Northwestern bastion of the Ku Klux Klan. (The KKK rapidly lost its steam when the state legislature repealed the 1844 law banning African Americans from the state in 1926.) The upside of Oregon's progressive tradition was the initiation of women's suffrage in 1912.

Portland changed overnight during World War II, when shipyards built by the Kaiser Company attracted 100,000 workers from the East. On September 30, 1942, *The Oregonian* ran a photograph of 100 New Yorkers disembarking from the "Magic Carpet Special" train. Some residents feared that there weren't enough services and housing for them all, and other Portlanders dredged up old racial animosities: "New Negro Migrants Worry City," ran another headline in *The Oregonian*.

Below: Shipyards and the Seattle skyline. A significant maritime link to Asia, Seattle was host to the 1999 meeting of the World Trade Organization.

The war was a mixed blessing for the region. Business boomed, but when President Franklin Delano Roosevelt ordered the removal of some 93,000 ethnic Japanese, including American citizens, from areas of imagined military significance, the Northwest—which had been passing discriminatory legislation against Asians for years—was chosen to house some of them in special "relocation" camps. Fears were not alleviated in June 1942, when a Japanese submarine surfaced just outside the Columbia River estuary and lobbed a 5.5-inch shell at a nineteenth-century relic, Fort Stevens. The shell missed, but it did establish Oregon as the only American state to be attacked during World War II. (Not until 1989 did the federal government apologize for its treatment of the Japanese-American population and initiate restitution for their losses of civil rights, including ownership of property.)

In other respects, World War II was a boom time for the Northwest. As Washington's and Oregon's populations increased by 30 percent, lumber, agricultural, and mining companies went into overdrive to meet the demand, and the region expanded beyond industries based on natural resources. Seattle's Boeing and Bremerton's Puget Sound Navy Yard established Washington as a defense center. In Portland, manufacturing doubled between 1940 and 1946.

The postwar Northwest grew considerably—a tribute to its popularity and a challenge to its environment. While Washington's population increased from 1,736,191 in 1940 to 2,853,214 in 1960, eight hydroelectric dams tamed the previously wild Columbia River. The Northwest continued to look up—in the

most literal sense. If there is one symbol of the region that has persisted, it is the 605-foot Space Needle that Seattle unveiled at the 1962 World's Fair. "Back when we were in school, if you wanted attention, you put up your hand," Seattle booster Joe Gandy told *The New York Times*. "This is what the Space Needle will do for the Fair and Seattle."

So the Northwest moved onward and upward, raising interesting questions for the region's future. The advice Northwesterners give visitors—"Visit our state of enchantment—but for heaven's sake, don't stay," in the words of the former Oregon governor Tom McCall—isn't being heeded. Will the hundreds and thousands of people still migrating there enjoy the same quality of life as the people who have lived in Oregon, Washington, and northern California for generations? It is a question that residents of the Northwest are determined to answer affirmatively.

Left: The state capital building in Salem, Oregon. Founded by Methodist missionary Jason Lee in 1840–1, the city opened the West's oldest university, at Willamette, the following year.

Overleaf: The Pacific Science Center and Space Needle in Seattle. Part of 1962's Century 21 Exposition, these great structures continue to embody a city that aspires to world recognition. Seattle also has teams in three major sports—basketball, baseball, and football.

WASHINGTON

SEATTLE AND PUGET SOUND

Seattle

Doc Maynard's Public House: offers walks to subterranean part of city condemned in 1907

Klondike Gold Rush National Historical Park: interpretive center for life of gold miners

Wing Luke Asian Museum: commemorative to Wing Chong Luke, champion of the Chinese community of the State; features historical exhibits and Asian folk art

Seattle Center/Space Needle: 500-foot high observation deck gives a 360-degree panorama

Discovery Park: active military base from the Spanish-American War until 1970; miles of wooded trails and beaches; offers excellent views

Nordic Heritage Museum: re-creates experience of a typical Scandinavian immigrant

Museum of History and Industry: local pioneer, aviation, and maritime exhibits; features an 1880s Seattle street scene; mementoes of the Alaskan gold rushes

Thomas Burke Memorial Washington State Museum: features anthropology, geology, and zoology; includes 25-foot totem poles and boats

Olympia

Capitol Group: area of architectural interest featuring the Legislative Building (offers guided tours), the Temple of Justice, and the State Capital Museum

Port Madison Indian Reservation: the Suquamish Museum of photographs and artifacts, and the grave of Chief Seathl

Steilacoom

Fort Steilacoom: renovated officers' houses from the 1850s

Historical Association Museum: local history and pioneer exhibits

Nathaniel Orr House: an 1857 wagon-making shop with original furnishings and artifacts

Port Gamble

Thompson House: a nineteenth-century mansion, rebuilt and restored to its original standard, as is the *Jackson House*

Historic Museum: exhibits on the history of Pope & Talbot, the town's founders, with artifacts and photographs

Tacoma

Fort Nisqually Historic Site: reconstruction of an 1833 fort built by the Hudson's Bay Company; includes living history museum and period demonstrations

Point Defiance Park: includes *Camp Six Logging Museum,* which replicates a logging camp and offers rides on an original 90-ton Shay steam locomotive; surrounded by woodland trails and fishing facilities

Whidbey Island

Museum: photographs and Native American artifacts

Ebey's Landing National Historic Reserve: 1880s rural historic district including farms, natural prairies, coastal beaches, and vistas of the Puget Sound, Cascade and Olympic Mountain ranges; offers fort tours and contains the historical museum in Coupeville

Fort Casey State Park: interpretive center exhibiting the history of coastal forts; offers lighthouse tours and panoramic views; camping facilities

North Cascades National Park

Beautiful landscape of peaks, ridges, waterfalls, and more than 300 glaciers; offers full range of outdoor activities and nature trails

San Juan Island National Historical Park

Lopez Island: tranquil landscape of rolling hills; offers good cycle trails

Orcas Island: largely consists of Moran State Park with hiking trails, dense forest, fields, lakes, and an observation tower on Mount Constitution at 2,409 feet

San Juan Island: forms Limekiln Point State Park, which offers killer-whale watching, tours, and cruises; also includes *Friday Harbor*, with a visitor center and historical museum, featuring photographs, artifacts, historical re-enactments, and interpretive walks

Ross Lake National Recreation Area
Area of scenic beauty offering a variety of outdoor activities including hiking, boating, climbing, horseback riding, and nature watching with a range of wayside exhibits

Bellingham
Lummi Island: ancient native hunting ground; wooded and rural, with tranquil beaches
Whatcom Museum of History and Art: Northwestern artworks, exhibits on exploration, logging industry, and native artifacts

Lake Chelan National Recreation Area
A deep lake in the Cascade Range with exhibits of natural history and tours; outdoor activities include hunting and fishing

OLYMPIC PENINSULA

Port Townsend
Jefferson County Historical Society: military memorabilia, native artifacts, historical photographs, and period homes
Fort Worden State Park: restored barracks, attractive architecture, and military museum

Olympic National Park
Massive area of unspoilt natural beauty comprising the Hoh, Quinault, and Queets River rainforests, the last of which boasts the world's tallest Douglas fir tree; beaches such as Ruby Beach with its garnet-colored sand; the Sol Duc Hot Springs; Hurricane Ridge, with peaks, glaciers, and panoramic views; various interpretive centers on ecology, geology, and history; a Pioneer Memorial Museum, including a homesteader's cabin, logging bunkhouse, and a replica Makah whaling canoe; and Neah Bay, a tiny fishing village and home to the Makah Nation, which contains a superb museum of native artifacts discovered in an ancient settlement during the Ozette dig of the '70s

Makah Cultural & Research Center
World's largest collection of Northwest Indian artifacts predating European contact

Hoquiam and Aberdeen
Aberdeen Historical Museum: photographs, logging equipment, and turn-of-the-twentieth-century furnishings
Arnold Polson Park and Museum: features Hoquiam's Castle, a fully restored 1897 Colonial Revival mansion turned museum of pictoral history of the Grays Harbor communities

SOUTHWESTERN WASHINGTON

Oysterville
Fort Canby State Park: features oldest lighthouse in Pacific Northwest and also the Lewis and Clark Interpretive Center, with slide shows and illustrations of the celebrated expedition; camping facilities available

Fort Columbia State Park
Includes the remains of one of three forts that constituted the harbor defense of the Columbia River 1896–1947, an interpretive center, and a museum of local history

Vancouver
Fort Vancouver National Historic Site: the original fort, largely destroyed by 1866, is a reconstructed stockade with chief factor's house; a visitor center with museum of archaeological artifacts, slide shows, talks, and living-history programs; and lectures, tours, and collections on the archaeological site still being excavated

Mount Rainier National Park
Preserved land around the highest peak in the Cascade Range, glacier-clad and 14,410 feet high; maintains stunning alpine wildflower meadows; offers wide range of outdoor activities including skiing, mountain climbing, and nature watching with over 300 miles of trails; also contains the *Longmire Visitor Center*, with a museum of the mountain's history

Mount Saint Helens National Volcanic Monument
Based around the volcano of the same name, the monument includes two visitor centers with scenic views of the still-steaming crater (last erupted 1980); a lava dome, and other volcanic features; Johnson Ridge Observatory is the most popular viewpoint, but the one at Windy Ridge is a more natural environment from which to view the destruction

CENTRAL WASHINGTON

Colville Reservation
Nespelem: site of the last days of Chief Joseph of the Nez Percé, whose grave is marked by the Chief Joseph Memorial in the reservation cemetery

Chelan
Situated on the banks of the largest national lake in the state, a beautiful glacial trough that stretches 55 miles into the Cascades; the community offers the *Lake Chelan Historical Museum*, with local historical artifacts and lithographs

Wenatchee

North Central Washington Museum: exhibits on pioneering history, geology, archaeological heritage, natural history, and fine arts

Cashmere

Chelan County Historical Museum: includes a renowned collection of ancient Northwestern archaeological finds, and the grounds of a pioneer village of nineteenth-century log cabins

Fort Simcoe State Park

Includes the original fort structures of the commanding officer's quarters, illustrating military life in the mid-nineteenth century; also incorporates the town of *Goldendale*, which contains the *Klickitat County Historical Society Museum* in a restored Victorian clifftop mansion with scenic views; and the *Maryhill Museum of Art*, featuring an internationally recognized collection of works by Rodin, Native American basketry, and a unique collection of antique chess sets, all in a highly scenic setting

Ellensburg

Olmstead Place State Park: original home of pioneer Samuel Olmstead, complete with his restored cabin and outbuildings; the complex is a working farm with tours and demonstrations of antique equipment and practices

EASTERN WASHINGTON

Grand Coulee Dam

The largest concrete structure in the world and the biggest producer of hydroelectricity; the area includes the *Coulee Dam National Recreation Area & Visitor Center*, with guided tours, films, watersports facilities, and centers for wildlife observation; and *Sun Lakes State Park*, an interpretive center containing historical exhibits, with scenic views of the prehistoric Dry Falls

Yakima

Yakima Valley Museum: Yakima crafts, clothing, and settlers' horse-drawn vehicles
Yakima Nation Museum: history of native practices and lifeways
Toppenish: the primary town on the Yakima Indian Reservation with a dramatic theater, research library, film showings, and historic murals known as "wall poetry"

Spokane

Riverfront Park: area of 100 acres, encompassing two islands in the Spokane River; includes a historic clock tower, restored traditional carousel, and a variety of interesting sculpture pieces
Spokane County Courthouse: Chateauesque-style 1895 structure
Cheney Cowles Museum: historical exhibitions and decorative arts

Cathedral of St. John the Evangelist: Gothic architecture, 49-bell carillon, guided tours, and regular concerts
Spokane House Interpretive Center: tells the story of Spokane House, the oldest building in the state, and the history of the Spokane Nation and settlers; features live re-enactments and demonstrations
Fort Spokane: restored nineteenth-century buildings of the last frontier army post in the Pacific Northwest

Republic

Old Toroda: remnants of mining settlements, as also found in the ghost town of *Bodie*
Steptoe Battlefield Memorial: a 25-foot granite monument to the battles of the U.S. Army and several native tribes; site of the last native victory in 1858
Steptoe Butte: outcrop of the Selkirk Mountains with panoramic view across wheatlands and Cascade Mountains

Pullman

Museum of Anthropology: within Washington State University; holds various international collections of ethnographic items, particularly the McWhorter Collection from the Columbia Plateau;
Forks Timber Museum: gardens and forest parks containing an authentic fire-lookout tower, logging camp artifacts, pioneer exhibits, and regional history; offers bus tours of the area

Dayton

Dayton Historical Depot: oldest existing railroad station in the state
Columbia County Courthouse: the oldest courthouse in Washington; Italianate interior with an extensive collection of historical photography

Walla Walla

Fort Walla Walla Museum Complex: contains a small pioneer village of sixteen original and replica structures dating from 1859; furnished with local heirlooms and over 26,000 artifacts telling the story of the Pacific Northwest
Whitman Mission National Historic Site: an 1840s Presbyterian mission whose founders, Marcus and Narcissa Whitman, were murdered by the local Cayuse in the Native American uprisings; the site has a visitor center, guided tours, displays and artifacts from the mission's history

Sacagawea State Park

Named in honor of the Shoshone female guide of the Lewis and Clark expedition; has an interpretive center, prehistoric artifacts, tours, hiking trails, and freshwater activities

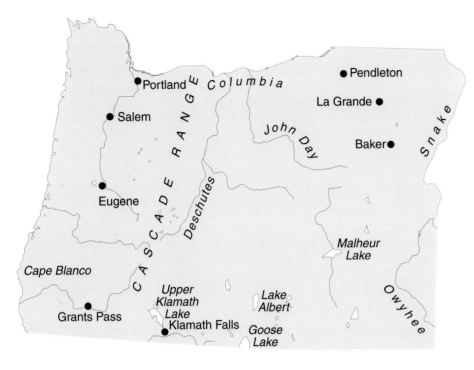

Bandon

Bullards Beach State Park: features unusual ancient rock formations and a small town with a historical museum

The Coos Bay Area

Coos County Historical Society Museum: exhibits of cultural heritage and industry through the pioneers, logging, and regional Indian crafts

Marshfield Sun Printing Museum: printing equipment and historical photographs housed in the original offices of the region's weekly newspaper, printed in the early twentieth century

Shore Acres State Park: formal estate gardens and spectacular ocean views

Oregon Dunes National Recreation Area: 44 miles of natural sand dunes; 30 lakes; hiking trails through wetlands, forests, and dunes; and a visitor center

OREGON

THE OREGON COAST

Astoria

Columbia River Maritime Museum: seven galleries depicting different aspects of Columbia's heritage—models, instruments, weapons, photographs, boats, and engines

Flavel House: 1885 Queen Anne mansion, now a museum with period furniture

Heritage Museum: 1904 Classical Revival building, formerly the city hall, exhibiting the region's history through Native American artifacts and local industries

Fort Clatsop National Memorial: reconstructed camp of Lewis and Clark (1805–06) including fort, canoe landing, and visitor center with slide shows and exhibits

Fort Stevens State Park: military reservation with fort; museum of maps, photographs, and artifacts; abandoned gun batteries; scenic views of Columbia River and the South Jetty; guided tours; miles of beaches, and camping facilities

Port Orford

Pretty and historic coastal town with forested mountains sweeping down to the sea

Siskiyou National Forest

Vast expanse of remote wilderness that can be explored by boat along the turbulent Rogue River

Florence

Old Town: late nineteenth-century fishing town remnants

Suislaw River Bridge & Pioneer Museum: Indian artifacts, logging equipment, and exhibits on early settlers

Newport

Burrows House Museum: an 1895 building that was originally a boarding house and a funeral parlor; now the Lincoln Historical Society Museum of natural history and research library

Log Cabin Museum: artifacts, maritime displays, and exhibits

Cape Foulweather: coastline state park and the highest point on the Oregon coast; a beautiful scenic point offering whale watching; discovered and named in 1778 by Captain James Cook

Tillamook County Pioneer Museum: a 1905 courthouse with over 35,000 artifacts and exhibits on early logging and cheesemaking, historical photographs, and a replica pioneer home

Seaside

Seaside Historical Museum: exhibits Clatsop Indian artifacts excavated in the '70s and the people's history; also includes the reconstructed salt works of the Lewis and Clark expedition

PORTLAND & SURROUNDING AREA

Downtown

Old Town Historic District: site of original settlement in 1843; architectural interest

New Market Theater: built in 1875, features original vendor stalls incorporated into the structure

Oregon History Center: exhibition of the state's history from prehistoric to present; maritime history, Western art, and architectural murals

Portland Art Museum: Northwest Coast native art, masks, textiles, sacred objects; European painting and sculpture; and a collection of Asian art

Southwest Portland

Washington Park: zoo established in 1880s; Rose Test Gardens; and formal Japanese gardens

World Forestry Center: exhibits a 70-foot "talking tree," forest management, resources, and products; also displays a collection of petrified wood

Hoyt Arboretum: 175 acres of Washington Park, with guided walks through a varied collection of trees and shrubs; also features the *Garden of Solace*, which honors Oregonians killed in Vietnam

Northwest Portland

Forest Park: 1,000-acre nature reserve and the largest urban wilderness park in America; overlooks the Willamette River

Pittock Mansion: a beautifully restored 1914 French Renaissance Revival mansion notable for its views of the city's two rivers and five peaks of the Cascade Range

The East Side

Oregon Museum of Science and Industry: six exhibit halls, education center, planetarium, and a 219-foot diesel electric submarine

Sauvie Island

Howell Territorial Park: restored mid-nineteenth-century residences, early orchard, and children's agricultural museum

Columbia River Gorge

Crown Point State Park: features one of Oregon's most beautiful sights—a series of spectacular waterfalls; also holds *Vista House*, a 1916 structure housing an interpretive center with exhibits and a small art gallery

Cascade Locks Museum: commemorates the locks built in 1896 with photographs and artifacts; features the first steam locomotive in the Northwest and historical photographs; river tours available

Fort Dalles Historical Museum: housed in restored part of an 1850 fort; contains native and pioneer artifacts and an original covered wagon

Mount Hood National Forest

The highest peak in Oregon offers ski lifts part of the way up; also the site of *Timberline Lodge*, the setting of Stanley Kubrick's film *The Shining*

WILLAMETTE RIVER VALLEY

Oregon City

End of the Oregon Trail Interpretive Center: illustrates the heritage and spirit of the people who traversed the Oregon Trail with pioneer exhibits, hands-on activities, and mixed-media theaters

Rose Farm: restored 1847 house where the first territorial legislature met; also displays the original land grant signed by Abraham Lincoln

Champoeg State Park

Originally a Calapooya Indian village site, now a log-cabin museum and visitor center with paintings, photographs, films, and lectures

McLoughlin House National Historic Site

Guided tours around the home of John McLoughlin, called the "Father of Oregon"

Salem

Mission Mill Village: complex of restored nineteenth-century buildings

Capitol Building: tours available through this tall structure of white Vermont marble, decorated with carvings and sculptures of pioneers

Albany

Monteith House: 1849 home to the town founders and therefore Albany's oldest structure—indeed, one of the oldest in Oregon; now a museum including the general store that the founders built into the house

Corvallis

Benton County Historical Museum: 1867 Georgian Revival brick building; displays include local history and culture, photography, and an extensive library

Eugene

University of Oregon: filled with buildings of architectural interest and has a well-known Museum of Art

Lane County Historical Museum: displays the region's history with pioneer artifacts, photographs, maps, and vehicles

Cottage Grove

Cottage Grove Historical Museum: features antique mining equipment, working mill models, and a nineteenth-century octagonal church with original stained glass windows

SOUTHWEST OREGON

Jacksonville

Jacksonville Museum of Southern Oregon History: housed in the restored 1880s county courthouse, contains exhibits on railroading, stoneware, photography, and local history; also has a children's museum with many hands-on exhibits

Ashland

Pacific Northwest Museum of Natural History: contains the oldest shoe ever discovered (10,000 years old) and North America's oldest house (9,400 years old); more generally, it surveys the ecosystems of the Pacific Northwest

Oregon Caves National Monument

Cave passages and intricate flowstone formations of the Siskiyou Mountains, surrounded by virgin forest; cave tours, hiking, and wildlife watching are available

CENTRAL OREGON

Klamath Falls

A natural wildlife refuge and bird sanctuary; encompasses the *Klamath County Museum* of geology, history, anthropology, and wildlife of the Klamath Basin; the *Favell Museum of Western Art and Indian Artifacts*, which features an extensive arrowhead collection of worldwide acclaim; and the *Fort Klamath Museum*, which contains a replica of an 1863 guardhouse and exhibits from the Modoc War

Crater Lake National Park

A deep, blue, and beautiful lake held in the shell of volcanic Mount Mazama, with a spectacular 33-mile rim drive around the edge; surrounded by mountains, volcanic peaks, and evergreen forests, the lake offers such freshwater activities as fishing and boat tours; also available are ranger talks, walks, wildlife watching, and hiking; set in the park, the *Lava Lands Visitor Center* contains dioramas depicting the volcanic activity that created the Cascade peaks and has a trail leading through the lava beds; the *Petersen Rock Gardens* contain statues and castles made of local petrified wood, belemnite, malachite, lava, and obsidian

Shaniko

A ghost town with many remnants of the original settlement preserved, including the much-photographed 1901 school building

EASTERN OREGON

Joseph

Wallowa County Museum: displays on Nez Percé and history
Nez Percé Indian Cemetery: historic burial ground

Hells Canyon National Recreation Area: the deepest canyon on the continent—1,000 feet deeper than the Grand Canyon—was the winter retreat of the Nez Percé; it contains the Nee-Me-Poo Trail, which traces the route of the Nez Percé as they were pushed out of the valley; there is a lookout tower at Hat Point; activities include hiking, horseback riding, boat trips, and wildlife watching

Wallowa Mountains and Lake

Remote area featuring the spectacular Mount Howard; offers a cable-car ride to the summit with magnificent views; also has facilities for camping and back-country hiking

Pendleton

Pendleton Underground: tour of the town's subterranean passages used during Prohibition as saloons, card rooms, and brothels
Pendleton Woolen Mills: demonstrates the famous local industry practices since 1909
Umatilla Indian Reservation: contains one of the Pacific Northwest's oldest Roman Catholic missions

John Day

Kam Wah Chung & Co. Museum: home/opium den/general store of a famed Chinese herbalist; shows the history of the town and the Chinese community from the gold-rush era
John Day Fossil Beds National Monument: more than 1,000 acres containing rich quantities of fossil vegetation and animal life; contains a fossil museum, laboratory, and exhibits; offers scenic views, trails, hiking, fishing, wildlife watching, and Ranger programs

Canyon

Grant County Historical Museum and Village: a 29-building village of authentic reconstructed units, shops and stables among others; displays artifacts from the gold-rush era, Native American culture, cowboy paraphernalia, and regional homesteads

Burns

Harney County Historical Museum: displays artifacts of pioneer life in the area

Lakeview

Schmink Memorial Museum: built on the site of a brewery, laundry, and wrecking yard; houses an extensive photography collection and pioneer artifacts from the mid-nineteenth century

Baker City

The Oregon Trail Regional Museum: displays of period clothing and industrial artifacts
Eastern Oregon Museum: c.10,000 artifacts including agricultural machinery, dolls, and restored furnishings
National Historical Oregon Trail Interpretive Center: more than 4 miles of well-preserved, original trails

NORTHERN CALIFORNIA

THE MONTEREY COAST

Carmel

Mission San Carlos Borromeo del Río Carmelo: restored 1797 mission of architectural beauty, with re-created rooms

Torr House and Hawk Tower: 1919 home of the poet Robinson Jeffers built with stones from all over the world, including some from the Great Wall of China

Point Lobos State Reserve: bird and animal sanctuary with a rich underwater habitat; opportunity for gray-whale watching

Seventeen Mile Drive: 1880s forest and coast road from Carmel to Pacific Grove; passes through the Del Monte Forest, famous golf courses, and elaborate houses

Point Piños Light: oldest continuously operating lighthouse (since 1855) on the West Coast

Hearst Castle

Northwest of San Luis Obispo, this is one of the most extravagant houses in the world; built in the 1920s, it boasts of many famous guests once entertained by newspaper magnate William Randolph Hearst; its elaborate and luxurious decoration includes objects imported from around the world; tours available

Monterey

Larkin House: restored to original 1830s condition, with period antiques

Colton Hall Museum: restored public school and town hall, exhibiting artifacts and re-creations of the town's history

Stevenson House: 1830s boarding house-turned-museum of Robert Louis Stevenson memorabilia

Royal Presidio Chapel of San Carlos de Borromeo: 1795 chapel with impressive façade

The Old Custom House: oldest public building in California, in service from 1820s; now a museum of its own history

California's First Theater: constructed by English sailor Jack Swan as a saloon and apartment house, this building opened in 1846 as a theater for Mexican War veterans

First Brick House in California: built 1846 by a settler with homemade bricks of fired clay—a new technique for the region

Presidio: One of the most historically significant sites in all California, this was a native village for millennia and subsequently a military-fort site through the Spanish, Mexican, and American eras. A U.S. army center since 1846, the area shows sites of Indian grinding, ceremonial rocks, and fort ruins. There is also a museum of the site's history.

Pacific House: an 1847 courthouse, rooming house, and then dance hall; now a good museum of local history and Native American artifacts

Monterey Bay Aquarium: one of the largest and most sophisticated in the world

San Juan Bautista

Mission San Juan Bautista: founded in 1797 and built directly on the San Andreas fault, the mission has been restored to its appearance in 1812, with several period rooms

San Juan Bautista State Historic Park: once the largest town in central California, San Juan Bautista contains several historic structures, including the restored 1840 Castro House and the 1858 Plaza Hotel

Santa Cruz

Santa Cruz Mission State Park: houses the reconstructed 1794 mission in a complex of several restored eighteenth-century adobes

Museum of Art and History: historical exhibits from prehistory to present day; collection of American art since 1945

Santa Cruz City Museum: exhibits on local natural history, tours, and interactive displays

The Roaring Camp and Big Trees Narrow-Gauge Railroad: 1880s steam-train tours along the San Lorenzo River canyon with 1920s-style passenger coaches

SAN FRANCISCO

Early Town Center
Portsmouth Square: original plaza of the city; leads to several historic buildings

Financial District
World of Economics Gallery: displays gold ore, silver and gold ingots, and gold-rush-era coins valued at over $1 million
Pacific Heritage Museum: exhibits Chinese contribution to early industry in the area and American influence on China and Japan

The Embarcadero
Ferry Building: 1898 gateway to the city, with a 235-foot tower

Market Street
Mechanics Monument: striking public sculpture by Douglas Tilden (1899) commemorates the founder of the first ironworks in the city; also marks the original shoreline
Old Mint: 1874 Greek Revival building and the oldest in the downtown area

Civic Center
City Hall: immense domed 1915 building containing the opera, ballet, symphony, and modern-art museums
War Memorial Opera House & Veterans Building: setting of the signature of the 1945 United Nations Charter and 1951 final peace treaty with Japan
San Francisco Museum of Modern Art: notable collection of West Coast artists' work
Society of California Pioneers: museum of Californian history from the gold-rush era to the Panama-Pacific International Exhibition of 1915; 50,000 historic photographs
Asian Art Museum: one of the largest collections of Asian paintings, sculptures, ceramics, and textiles in the Western world

Nob Hill
Grace Cathedral: medieval-style building containing a strong collection of religious art and a 44-bell carillon
San Francisco Cable Car Museum: demonstrates the workings of the cable car with portions from some of the earliest examples, including the prototype

Chinatown
Old St. Mary's Church: served as the bishop's seat until 1891
Chinese Consolidated Benevolent Building: headquarters of the Six Companies that brought laborers into the city, mid-nineteenth century
Chinese Historical Society of America: photographs, artifacts, and memorabilia on the Chinese presence in the United States

North Beach
Contains the city's oldest Roman Catholic parish church

Telegraph Hill
Coit Tower: 540 feet above the bay, providing good panoramic views; also houses 16 Public Art Project murals depicting scenes of California life

West of Van Ness
First Unitarian Church: built in 1888; contains some interesting carving and sculptures
Haas-Lilienthal House: built in 1886; striking Victorian architecture; offers walking tours of the Pacific Heights
Swedenborgian Church of the New Jerusalem: an 1895 building combining Italian and California architecture; notable for its ornamentation and grounds
California Historical Society Museum: historical exhibits and impressive collection of paintings and rare prints

Cow Hollow
Octagon House: example of interesting architectural theory; exhibits decorative artwork
Vedanta Old Temple: early twentieth century temple architecturally designed in a variety of international styles to express the belief that all religions have validity
San Francisco Fire Department Memorial Museum: historical photographs and fire equipment, including an 1810 fire engine

The Waterfront
Alcatraz: famous island long used as a prison; accessible by ferry
Angel Island: state park with ghostly military ruins and a visitor center explaining the history of the island
San Francisco Maritime National Historic Park: collection of ships' models, photographs, and memorabilia; also access to a number of restored vintage ships moored on the waterfront at Hyde Street Pier
Fort Mason: demilitarized fort containing studios, and restaurants; hosts periodic cultural events; also houses several museums including the *San Francisco Craft and Folk Art Museum*
Palace of Fine Arts: last remnant of the 1915 Panama-Pacific International Exhibition, reconstructed here; houses the *Exploratorium* science museum with 650 hands-on exhibits
The Presidio: the oldest continuously occupied army base in the western United States; houses a museum displaying armaments and uniforms; offers access to trails, beaches, forest, and grassland
Fort Point National Historic Site: mid-nineteenth-century fortification below the Golden Gate Bridge; houses numerous Civil War memorabilia; offers tours, short films, and military drills
California Palace of the Legion of Honor: museum of French fine and decorative arts, including medieval tapestries

Cliff House: gives spectacular views of the coast; visitor center

Golden Gate Bridge: landmark 1937 suspension bridge—third-longest in the world

Golden Gate National Recreation Area: offers views of San Francisco across the mouth of the bay; contains remains of three twentieth-century forts; offers tours of Alcatraz, hiking, and cultural programs

Golden Gate Park: renowned urban park with groves, lawns, lakes, ponds, and cultural amenities; notable for its horticultural diversity and conservatory of flowers

M. H. de Young Memorial Museum: mid-nineteenth-century and earlier European, American, folk, and primitive art; also houses the *Asian Art Museum of San Francisco* with pieces from every major Asian civilization and a large collection of Chinese jade

Mission

Mission Dolores (or San Francisco de Asis): Restored 1776 mission with a museum of relics and manuscripts

THE EAST BAY

Oakland

First and Last Chance Saloon: historical bar, opened in 1883, and built from timbers of an old whaling ship; maintained in its original state; displays numerous monuments to its history

The Oakland Museum: displays artifacts, tools, clothing, wagons, a restored gold-rush assayer's office, natural history, and a renowned collection of California art and photography

Joaquin Miller Park: contains the various and unusual homes of the poet and dramatist Joaquin Miller

Mormon Temple: offers fine views of the bay area

Berkeley

Phoebe Hearst Museum of Anthropology: on campus of the university; huge collection of Native American, Inuit, and Polynesian artifacts

Takora Sake Tasting Room: sampling of sake from one of the largest producers in Japan

Concord

Port Chicago Naval Magazine National Memorial: site of the worst World War II-related disaster in the state—a huge explosion in 1944 in the Concord Weapons Station; there are tours of the port, the Port Chicago Museum, and the memorial chapel

Martinez

John Muir National Historic Site: offers guided tours around the home of conservationist John Muir, with family memorabilia and films that show Muir's contribution to the founding of Yosemite National Park

Treasure Island

Constructed in 1936, and a naval base from 1941–97, this island houses a museum of the 1939 World's Fair and has memorable views of the San Francisco skyline

Danville

Eugene O'Neill National Historic Site: guided tours around Tao House, home of the renowned playwright

NORTH BAY

Benicia

First State Capitol: used in 1852 for just thirteen months, restored as a museum and furnished in the legislative style of the time

Benicia Historical Museum: exhibits and displays on local history

Mount Diablo State Park

Conserves Mount Diablo, nearly 14,000 feet high, with views from the summit of up to 10,200 miles in all directions

THE PENINSULA

Año Nuevo Stae Reserve

Beautiful natural site with guided tours to observe northern elephant seals, gray whales, and birds

Pacifica

Sweeney Ridge: historic site from which the Spanish first saw San Francisco Bay in 1769

Sánchez Adobe: Hispanic-period adobe house, completed in 1846; used variously as a speakeasy, a brothel, and an artichoke warehouse; since restored as a museum with period furnishings

Belmont

Ralston Hall: home of the founder of the Bank of California; luxurious mansion restored to its 1864 grandeur

Woodside

Filoli: 1916 Georgian-style house with acclaimed estate gardens

Stanford University

Stanford University Museum of Art: large collections of international art, photographic studies, Rodin sculptures, and the golden spike that marked the completion of the first transcontinental railroad

San Jose Area

Winchester Mystery House: built and continuously adapted from 1884 until 1922 due to a superstitious belief that if building ceased, the owner would die

San Jose Historical Museum: historical and cultural collections from the Spanish/Mexican period among others; offers walking tours of historic San Jose

Luis María Peralta Adobe: constructed before 1800 by the first settlers; contains replica Mission-period furnishings

New Almaden Quicksilver County Park and Museum: site of the largest mercury mine in America; museum of mining artifacts

Mission Santa Clara de Asís: replica of 1825 church on site of a 1777 mission; impressive ceiling designs

Mission San Jose de Guadalupe: replica of a 1797 mission, famous for its Native American orchestra; museum of mission artifacts

Rosicrucian Museum: designed in the rare Ancient-Egyptian style; houses a huge collection of Assyrian and Babylonian artifacts

WINE COUNTRY

Napa Valley

Has over 300 wineries, most of which offer free tastings

Sonoma

Sonoma State Historic Park: contains Sonoma Plaza—setting for the major act of the Bear Flag Revolt that pushed California toward American control; also contains restored historic homes including ***Lachryma Montis***—1850s home of General Vallejo—and the ***Buena Vista Winery,*** the oldest premium winery in the state

Petaluma

Petaluma Adobe: one of the oldest preserved buildings in northern California, it was the largest and richest privately owned Mexican estate north of San Francisco Bay; visitors may see the extensive headquarters of this large, self-sufficient ranch with its displays of Mexican period artifacts

Santa Rosa

Luther Burbank Home and Gardens: two-acre memorial garden and restored house of the dedicated horticulturalist; museum of Burbank's life and work

Jack London State Historic Park

Contains burnt-out remains of London's 1911 mansion in Glen Ellen and a museum dedicated to the adventurous writer and his life

Saint Helena

Bale Grist Mill State Historic Park: site of a large wooden mill wheel built in 1846

Silverado Museum: dedicated to the Scottish novelist and poet Robert Louis Stevenson, with a collection of original manuscripts, first editions, and memorabilia

Calistoga

Robert Louis Stevenson State Park: comprises the upper parts of the 4,500-foot ***Mount Saint Helena***; marks the place of Stevenson's honeymoon with his American wife; paths to the summit with spectacular views

Old Faithful Geyser of California: boiling water jets 60 feet into the air, in a region of petrified forests, some of which are the largest of their kind

Healdsburg

Healdsburg Museum: Pomo Indian basketry, antique firearms, and many other local cultural artifacts

THE SACRAMENTO VALLEY

Sacramento

Old Sacramento: contains historic sites including the restored 1855 courtroom and a communications museum

California State Railroad Museum: interpretive exhibits on the history of rail travel in California and the West; also houses the reconstructed Central Pacific Railroad headquarters, the Passenger Station, and the Freight Depot

California State Indian Museum: craft objects and photographs celebrate the heritage of native Californian culture

Crocker Art Gallery: European Renaissance and later artworks, including contemporary and Californian examples

California State Capitol: restored Renaissance Revival capitol building and state offices, completed in 1894 at a cost of 2.4 million dollars; many historic rooms are open to the public and show exhibits of the building's history

Sutter's Fort: an original 1840 fort and reconstructed compound with museum of gold-rush relics

Oroville

Chinese Temple: opened in 1863 to serve some 10,000 local Chinese residents; now a museum of Chinese artifacts and craft with extensive and priceless displays of tapestries and costumes; also boasts a magnificent meditation garden

THE INLAND NORTH

Weaverville

Weaverville Joss House: a Taoist temple, now a state park, preserved exactly as it was over a hundred years ago with imported Chinese tapestries and altars; the oldest still in use in California, built in 1874 after the destruction of previous structures on the site

LaGrange Mine: remnants of one of the largest hydraulic gold mines in the world; first operated c.1862

Shasta State Historic Park

Shasta: ruined town that was once the county seat and most prominent settlement; restored jail and courthouse with period relics

Shasta-Trinity National Forests: surround **Mount Shasta**, a 14,162-foot peak of the Cascade Range which has facilities for climbing and hiking

Whiskytown-Shasta-Trinity National Recreation Area: Whiskytown Lake and the surrounding extensive backcountry offers a host of water-related activities, hunting, horseback riding, and interpretive programs

Siskiyou County Museum: Native, gold-rush, and later artifacts; restored miners' cabins; an original mine shaft

Lava Beds National Monument

"Captain Jack's Stronghold": historic lava-tube cave network used by the Modoc leader Kintpuash, called "Captain Jack," and his followers; interpretive talks and cave explorations

Modoc County Museum: Native artifacts and firearms from the fifteenth century to World War II

Fandango Pass and Fort Bidwell

Fort remains, now an Indian reservation; road access to 6,100-foot Fandango Pass, a historic crossing to the gold fields of Sacramento

Lassen Volcanic National Park

Contains Lassen Peak, an active plug-dome volcano; hot springs; large lava pinnacles; huge mountains created by lava flow, jagged craters, and steaming sulphur vents; for visitors, there are interpretive programs, nature walks, hiking, skiing, boating, and winter sports

GOLD RUSH COUNTRY

Plumas-Eureka State Park

A park of scenic beauty, it contains a museum of mining artifacts, a stamp mill, a restored bushman mill, a working blacksmith shop from 1900, and the site of the original ski area (1860)

Nevada City

Miners Foundry Culture Center: collection of Victoriana in an enormous 1856 building

Nevada County Historical Society Museum: contains a Chinese joss house and native exhibits

Grass Valley

North Star Mining Museum: exhibits on gold mining from the 1880s, including the largest pelton wheel ever constructed

Empire Mine State Historical Park: guided tours down main shaft of the oldest, richest, and deepest mine in California; set in a picturesque forested area

Auburn

Gold Country Museum: exhibits on all major mining techniques, working models, and later industries; exhibits on the gold rush; tours down a mine shaft; and gold panning

Marshall Gold Discovery State Historic Park

Memorializes the area where the gold rush began after James Marshall discovered gold here in 1848; includes Sutter's Mill replica, Marshall's cabin, and a museum displaying local history; contains *Marshall's Grave*, marked by an 1889 statue of him pointing to the site of the first gold flake found; also offers living history programs and gold panning

Placerville

El Dorado County Historical Museum: gold-rush artifacts, ranching and logging equipment, and a collection of rolling stock

Hangtown Gold Bug Park: two shafts of a hard-rock gold mine open for tours, running 350 feet into the hillside

Fiddletown: historic town with the *Chew Kee Store*, 1850 Chinese herbalist shop with original furnishings

Indian Grinding Rock State Park

Located in the Sierra Nevada foothills, the park preserves an enormous Miwok grinding rock; includes a cultural center of Miwok craft; a reconstructed Miwok village; and the *Chaw'se Regional Indian Museum*, containing artifacts from the Sierra Nevada area

Jackson

Kennedy Tailing Wheels Park: Argonaut Mine with 58-foot-diameter tailing wheels from 1912

Amador County Museum: built in 1859 by one of the first settlers in the area, it contains mining models, artifacts, and Miwok basketry

Murphys

Murphys Hotel: restored 1856 hotel that includes Mark Twain among its notable guests

Old Timers Museum: local historical artifacts from the gold-rush era onward

Angels Camp

A traditional gold-rush town that hosts an annual frog jump to celebrate Mark Twain's stay, at the *Hotel Angels*, and his short story "The Celebrated Jumping Frog of Calaveras County"

Sonora

A logging town with numerous Victorian houses and false-fronted buildings

Columbia State Historic Park

Site of a fully restored gold-rush town, Columbia, founded in 1850, which was the state's second largest city by 1854; offers stagecoach rides around the town

Coulterville

Jeffrey Hotel: restored 1856 hotel, originally a Mexican dance hall

Sun Sun Wo Store: restored early 1850s Chinese general store still stocked with supplies

Hornitos

Ghost town founded by Mexicans, which, during its heyday, held c.15,000 residents; contains an old jailhouse, Wells Fargo office, and general store

Mariposa

Northern Mariposa History Center: demonstrates the history of mining with a full-size working stamp mill and a reconstructed Miwok village; also gives craft demonstrations

California State Mining and Mineral Museum: large displays of mineral samples and exhibits of mining practices

THE SIERRA NEVADA

Lake Tahoe

One of the highest, largest, deepest, and coldest lakes in the world; more than 1,000 feet deep

Tahoe City: on the northwestern shore, contains the *Gatekeeper's Museum* full of nineteenth-century artifacts and Native American basketry

Mariposa Grove: contains *Eagle's Rock,* which offers panoramic views of the lake

Donner Pass

Donner Memorial State Park: holds the *Emigrant Trail Museum*, which contains artifacts of the pioneers who traveled through the area and a history of their tragedy in 1846

Yosemite National Park

An expanse of alpine wilderness, Giant Sequoia groves, and Yosemite Valley; includes the famous Bridal Veil Falls and Glacier Point; offers a range of outdoor activities, cultural demonstrations, tours, and natural history seminars; also includes the *Indian Cultural Museum*, containing dioramas of Miwok life and craft exhibits; the *El Portal Transportation Exhibit*, with material from the Yosemite Valley Railroad; and the *Pioneer Yosemite History Center*, with reconstructed period buildings and structures

Bodie

One of the West's most complete ghost towns; with a one-time population of 10,000, it was a boom town in 1877 and infamous for its wild living; contains mainly wooden buildings from the period, when every other building on the main street was a saloon, supplied by seven breweries; a museum gives the local history

Independence

Eastern California Museum: describes life in nearby Japanese relocation camp of World War II with photos and artifacts; also local history, botany, geology, and native basketry

Manzanar National Historic Site: contains visible remains of the Manzanar War Relocation Center of World War II, constructed to intern various immigrant communities to prevent "security risks"

Grass Valley

The most prosperous and substantial of the gold-mining towns; attractions include the **North Star Mining Museum and Empire Mine**, which is preserved as a state park

Nevada City

Old Firehouse: restored museum of local and social history

Downieville

A town set in the most rugged and beautiful part of the region, full of waterfalls and forests

THE SAN JOAQUIN VALLEY

Devils Postpile National Monument

A fine example of columnar jointed basalt; also setting for the 101-foot-high "Rainbow Falls"; trails, hiking, and fishing are available

Tehachapi Pass

Tehachapi Loop: a great feat of railroad engineering, completed in 1876; the busiest single-tracked mainline in the world and a very scenic point

Fort Tejon

Reconstructed U.S. Army outpost established in 1854; museum of period life and artifacts

Bakersfield

The Kern County Museum: over sixty restored nineteenth-century buildings from the area moved to this location

Teft

West Kern Oil Museum: chronicles the history of the petroleum industry; original equipment and informative displays and fossils

Colonel Allensworth State Historic Park

Visitor center with interpretive exhibits and films; restored buildings, including the school, in the only California town to be founded, financed, and governed by African Americans

Fresno

Meux Home Museum: restored, ornate 1880s house displaying the period, featuring craft demonstrations and guided tours

Fresno Metropolitan Museum: art, hands-on science exhibits, collections of antique puzzles, Chinese artifacts, and historical displays

Stockton

Haggin Museum: local history and industry; American and French paintings; native crafts; re-creation of a turn-of-the-century California town

Lodi

San Joaquin County Historical Museum: early twentieth-century artifacts and original and re-created rooms and shops; living history programs

THE NORTH COAST

Marin County

Sausalito: features the **Bay Area Discovery Museum**, a hands-on children's museum aimed at explaining the area's aquatic ecosystem, with an underwater sea tunnel, an aquarium, and a fishing pier

Mill Valley: 1890s suburban development with many historic buildings, including a restored 1836 sawmill

Muir Woods National Monument: preserved giant redwood forests with paved trails

China Camp State Park: preserved remnants of more than two dozen Chinese shrimping villages

Mission San Rafael Arcangel

Reconstructed 1870s mission with original features from an 1817 auxiliary that stood on the site

Point Reyes National Seashore

Bear Valley Visitor Center: provides information about the peninsula and also shows a reconstructed Miwok village

Earthquake Trail: a rift in the earth along the San Andreas fault

Point Reyes Bird Observatory: a research and study center open for tours

Fort Ross

A striking and dramatic reconstructed 1812 Russian settlement with a log-house and Orthodox chapel

Mendocino

Kelley House Museum: 1861 pioneer's home containing artifacts and photographs of the lumbering and shipping industries; offers tours of sea caves

Eureka

Old Town: preserves much of its Victorian architecture, especially in the **Living History Museum** of the Victorian experience

Fort Humboldt State Historic Park: preserves 1853 fort remains; visitor center with interpretive exhibits

Willow Creek

Self-titled "Gateway to Bigfoot Country," with a visitor center explaining the legendary phenomenon of the gigantic wild man

Crescent City

Redwood National Park: holds an abundant diversity of wildlife and huge redwood trees, ancient monuments of the prehistoric past; facilities include hiking; bird-, elk-, and whale-watching, horseback riding, tidepool walks, ranger talks, and guided kayak programs